# Mother's Ruin

The extraordinary true story of how alcohol
destroys a family

## NICOLA BARRY

headline
review

First published in 2007 by HEADLINE REVIEW
An imprint of Headline Publishing Group

First published in paperback in 2008
by HEADLINE REVIEW

1

Cataloguing in Publication Data is available from the British Library

978 0 7553 1674 8

Typeset in Dante by Avon DataSet Ltd,
Bidford-on-Avon, Warwickshire

Printed and bound in Great Britain by Clays Ltd, St Ives plc

Headline's policy is to use papers that are natural, renewable and recyclable
products and made from wood grown in sustainable forests. The logging and
manufacturing processes are expected to conform to the environmental
regulations of the country of origin.

HEADLINE PUBLISHING GROUP
An Hachette Livre UK Company
338 Euston Road
London NW1 3BH

www.reviewbooks.co.uk
www.headline.co.uk

To Alastair

*A little onward lend thy guiding hand*
*To these dark steps, a little further on.*
John Milton

# Contents

Acknowledgements ix

Preface 1

1 Falling from Grace 9

2 A Price for Everything 39

3 Worn Out and Wasted 49

4 Edge of Society 69

5 Envy and Shame 93

6 Road to Despair 107

7 Stolen Moments 131

8 Forgive Me, Mother 163

9 Falling Down Drunk 171

10 Like Mother, Like Daughter 195

11 Naked but Not Ashamed 229

12 Death's Door 253

13 Last Rites 269

Afterword 285

# Acknowledgements

I would like to thank Professor Willy Maley of Glasgow University's Creative Writing course, for being such a brilliant mentor and motivator. More recently, Dr Andrew Radford of the same department has guided and encouraged me as well. I am also grateful to my fellow creative writing students for the many hours they spent agonising over my efforts.

Also, *Press and Journal* sub-editors, Tom Forsyth and Isabelle Morgan, who kept me going by telling me that, one day, someone would take on this book.

I owe a debt of gratitude to my agent, Jenny Brown, who never lost hope and line editor, Ann Lloyd, for dotting every 'i' and crossing every 't' as well as to Headline editor, Andrea Henry, who has been the personification of charm and patience throughout this whole lengthy process.

On a more personal level, I am grateful to Lesley

McRobb and my Florida friends Brenda Cosentino and the Martini Girls, Marianne and the two Joyces, for so willingly poring over my scribblings. And to Sister Margaret for her spiritual sustenance and precious love.

A big thank you to Alastair for the constant supply of humour, tea and nagging and his wonderful daughters, Joanne and Hazel, for accepting me as their wicked stepmother, even though I arrived with the baggage of an entire psychiatric convention.

Last, but not least, I wish to thank my West Highland Terrier, Coll, who lay beside me as I wrote, never averse to a quick cuddle or an inspirational game of tugger whenever the muse took a tea break.

# Preface

I was born drunk. I lay screaming on the delivery table, blowing out alcohol fumes as if my life depended on the stuff, the smell so strong a theatre sister asked who'd been drinking – so my mother told me, years later.

The sister, looking irate as she asked the question, peered into the masked faces surrounding her, accusing, angry. Nobody said a word. The nurses eyed each other, unsure how to respond, yet no one could dispute the existence of the smell.

My mother had tippled gin the night before, to calm her nerves. Being a doctor, she had the decency to cut down in time for my arrival but couldn't bear to stop right through the pregnancy. It was hard enough for her to stop during the labour, although the gas and air must have helped take her mind off the awful fact of her temporary sobriety.

My father told me she'd been drunk on the way home from the Edinburgh Royal Infirmary a few days later. As a consultant anaesthetist, he agonised about how his wife had managed to drink on the ward and whether anyone had seen her – perhaps one of his colleagues.

I know how she managed. Whenever I went to hospital for operations on my legs, years later, my mother would tell me, yet again, how she had half filled a bottle of orange juice with vodka and kept it on her locker, sipping from it every so often, her mood cheerier by the hour. You'd think the staff would have noticed but, as she said herself, the medical profession never suspected one of their own.

What my father didn't tell me was how, driving her back home from the maternity ward, he'd smelled her breath, stopped the car and dragged her out onto the road. She told me that bit, just one of many tales of his frequent rages. She said he never hit her, not physically anyway; but, she reckoned, if she ever did leave him, she'd have been able to divorce him on the grounds of mental cruelty.

'You useless bloody woman,' he'd bellowed that day, pulling her out of the car and shaking her shoulders. 'Can't stay sober long enough to have a bloody baby.'

'I know what I'm doing,' she shouted back. 'I'm a doctor, too, you know.'

That was how they went on all the time, my parents.

She was terrified of him and drank because of his shouting, and he shouted because of her drinking. No one could remember which had come first, but together they were a five-star disaster.

Looking back, I suppose Mummy was lucky her drinking didn't cause me brain damage. She'd been relatively sober at the birth of my three brothers – so she said. She'd been a social drinker in those days, knew how to control it. It was years before I realised that people who talked about being able to control their drinking usually had a problem with it.

As it was, my parents argued about whether her drinking during pregnancy had caused the condition in my hips, bilateral slipped epiphysis, the effects of which haunted me for years. I never heard them ask one of the doctors, but my father was convinced it was caused by Foetal Alcohol Syndrome and used it as yet another stick with which to beat her.

Mothers and babes are supposed to bond early on. She and I did bond, after a fashion, in as much as you can bond with someone who's permanently pissed. Alcohol was the glue that held us together, mother and I. Bloody Marys are thicker than water, after all. We loved each other a lot more than we realised while she was alive. The trouble was she needed so much looking after that neither of us knew which one was the parent and which the child.

Throughout my early childhood, it seemed she knew what she was doing with drink. I never noticed anything was particularly amiss until the day, at the age of ten, I ended up in a wheelchair, after slipping on ice outside the house, while making a slide for one of my brothers. Both my legs broke at the hip and I couldn't walk.

Mummy did her best but, like so many doctors, she just wasn't cut out for hands-on care. She always had a drink before helping me onto a commode, for example. Indeed, she couldn't face any nursing tasks without 'a wee cocktail', her way of acknowledging she'd had a slug out of the bottle. At that stage, I wouldn't have said she was an alcoholic. She saw nursing as beneath her. She wanted to be out having a good time and wasn't. I was in the way. But she was far too kind to admit such a lack of maternal feeling.

My father's barely developed paternal feelings shrank even further after my initial hospitalisation. 'Bloody crippled idiot,' he'd mutter under his breath, thinking I wouldn't hear. He used to leave the house in the morning, slam the front door until the glass cracked the whole way down, and then walk along the path to his car, shouting and swearing to himself until he was out of earshot: 'Bloody this', 'Bloody that', 'Bloody crippled fool' and 'Bloody drunken imbecile.'

Then, all of a sudden, when I was ten and 'wheelchair-bound', my mother was forever pouring herself a drink –

every time she had to bring me a bedpan, give me a bed bath or speak to my surgeon. Maybe she had always helped herself to gin and tonic like this. Maybe I was only noticing because we were in such close proximity. Even when she switched to vodka and tonic, which she believed didn't smell, I could tell, and smell, a mile away. 'You should be a detective when you grow up, Nic,' she'd say, hurt creeping into her voice, if I ever accused her of being drunk.

One of us always managed to be there for the other, nevertheless. When I was helpless on the floor, she'd stuff a fag into her mouth and try to haul me back up into the chair. When she was helpless on the floor, I would try to do the same for her. We were a team, like synchronised swimmers without the water. No matter how drunk she was, I could make her move. Just two words sufficed: 'Daddy's coming.'

By the time I was twelve, my mother was a chronic alcoholic. I soon learned from my three older brothers that I had to grow up quickly or not at all. To say her drinking ruined my life would be a cop-out – ruled my life is more like it. I watched her drink from the bottle until, one day, the tables turned and the bottle began to drink her; all of her. In a matter of months, she turned from being a strikingly beautiful woman into a pickled old prune, her youth sucked utterly dry. It was as if the familiar mother had died and a new one – older, more uncertain – had taken her place; one prone to staggeringly sudden changes of mood.

We children were left to get on with it. My three brothers were over-anxious, seriously depressed at times. Yet they were all survivors at the end of the day, apart, perhaps, from Richard. We developed our own coping mechanisms. I chewed my thumbnails and the surrounding skin until my hands bled. I chewed as I watched TV, when I read or while listening to my parents argue. The act of chewing my skin, hurting my own flesh, was the only way I could feel relaxed. I went on doing this through adulthood, until I met Alastair, my partner of ten years, without realising the clinical name for it was 'deliberate self-harm', a condition common in young people who, for example, cut themselves with razors as a way of releasing pent-up feelings of self-loathing.

I developed a habit of banging my head in the way children in Romanian orphanages sometimes do after years of neglect. I did it when I was sitting anywhere, especially in the car. I could bang my head the whole way from Edinburgh to London. If Mummy was drunk in the front of the car and Daddy was shouting, I'd bang and sing so loudly that it drowned out everything else.

I also rolled in bed at night in order to get to sleep, rolling from side to side, sometimes with real violence so that my bed would travel noisily across the linoleum like a small boat cutting through the swell of a rough sea. I thought it quite normal. Again, it was only as an adult that I realised that this was yet another sign of dysfunction, known as Rhythmic Movement Disorder. It persisted until, at eleven, I was sent away to school.

As for drinking, I started really young, heading exactly the same way as my mother; drinking simply because there were so many things I couldn't face. Eating out was especially hard; in fact, mixing with other people required a big drink beforehand, at least a bottle of wine.

'Drink affects you really quickly,' they'd say, unaware that I had stocked up before leaving the house.

Soon, everything became an excuse for a drink. By seventeen, I couldn't even dry my hair without a glass of something in my hand. I never acknowledged the mess it would make of me.

Yet, in a sense, I was privileged. For years I had the opportunity to watch as booze stripped my mother of her face, figure, friends and life. I knew perfectly well that drink is a horrible way to live and quickly learned that it's an even more miserable way to die. Nevertheless, I let it set about destroying me as well.

Nobody really knew what went on in our house. We didn't just hide the truth from other people but from each other, as well. That was our tragedy. We lived separately but together, sneaking around, children sniffing their mother's breath for clues. There were bottles hidden everywhere in our house: full ones, empty ones, bottles long forgotten, never opened. We didn't live but existed in a mausoleum of our own making. Yet, miserable as it was, I hated it when our desperate edifice fell apart. We all did. We'd kept it together so long, nurturing our very own oasis of insanity. Only when we ventured out into the world did we realise how mad we really were. For most children, it is strangers in the world outside who may bring danger. For us, the danger was right there in the house, under our feet, just waiting to trip us up.

# Chapter 1

# Falling from Grace

It always happened in the evenings, when I was alone with her. As usual, my brothers were away at school and my father would be out at the hospital – saving lives being more important than staying with us. If he could volunteer to be on duty, he would. Otherwise, mountain climbing provided him with a suitable means of escape.

I'd hear her calling my name.

'Nicola . . . Nicola . . .' Softly at first, then louder and louder. 'N . . . i . . . c . . . o . . . l . . . a . . .'

My face flushes with anger and my hands start trembling. 'Not tonight,' I think. 'Please God, not tonight.'

'N . . . i . . . c . . . o . . . l . . . a . . .'

It comes out in a long, loud wail. People outside in the street must be able to hear her screeching.

I get to my feet and turn up the telly until it's at full

blast. The neighbours must wonder what the hell goes on in our house: night after night, this weird combination of sound effects. I try to concentrate on the film, a love story of sorts. All I can see are characters who mean nothing to me flickering across the screen. That was the trouble with our house. You couldn't enjoy a film on telly or get caught up in a book because there was always this sideshow in the background, this ongoing saga, far more unpredictable than anything produced for the box.

Because the neighbours were well bred and polite, nobody ever said anything when Mummy staggered out in the mornings, her black leather shopping bag full of rattling empties. They thought plenty but said nothing. They knew, of course, she was going to dispose of them, as furtively as she could, to hide them from Daddy, from us and from the GP who occasionally called in the hope of catching her off guard. She was too careful for him. No, she had not been drinking. He could have her word. Anyway, if we were so sure and so clever, where was the evidence?

Nor did anyone ever say anything when they saw her coming back from the shops, about the way she hurried up the road, a look of fixed concentration on her face, a lonely, hunted woman making her way back to a prison of her own choosing, clutching the same shopping bag, this time with a full bottle or two. She would get to our front door and lurch inside, and nobody would see her again until the following morning. That was our life: her, our, life. As long as nobody knew what was going on, or at least pretended they didn't, then she could do what she liked, drink herself to death if she wanted to. That is the penalty of respectability.

Daddy was right. Had we not been so bloody middle class, social workers would have intervened years ago.

'N . . . i . . . c . . . o . . . l . . . a . . .'

Where is her voice coming from this time? Is she in the bathroom next to her bedroom on the first floor? Or in bed? Our house, in a terrace, consisted of three floors. Nobody slept on the top floor except when we had lodgers. I slept in a small room, badly in need of a coat of fresh paint, next to my mother's, and my father had his own bedroom along the hallway. His room was dark, full of antique furniture covered in hideously patterned throws. He did everything in his room: slept, read, listened to music, only emerging to work and eat – which he sometimes deigned to do around the table in the downstairs dining room, with us.

'N . . . i . . . c . . . o . . . l . . . a . . .'

Please don't let her be in the bath. I close my eyes to listen for creaks. Her bedroom floor creaks like an old garden gate. There is no sound. I have a horrible feeling she's in the bath and dread the thought of fishing her out. I am always fishing her out of the bath. Soaking in warm water seemed to make her feel normal, even though she would have had a good drink first. She's always drunk when she takes a bath. Sometimes she leaves the taps running, returns to her room for a few slugs of spirit and forgets about the bath. As a result, the black and yellow linoleum on the bathroom floor is damp and rotting in places where the water has overrun and seeped through to the ceiling over the room below, one we never really use other than for the occasional Christmas dinner. There are dark, fungal patches in every corner of that ceiling; all so similar they could have been deliberately chosen as decoration, a touch of art nouveau. Mind you, there are patches on the paintwork throughout the house, chips in all the wood and worn carpets with mice running between the rooms, darting behind cupboards and wardrobes.

When I hear Mummy call again, I give in, wearily climb the stairs. Through the half-closed bathroom door, I can hear her retching, splashing about in the bath as if she's enjoying herself, but I know she's really struggling to stand up. I open the door and see her grubby dressing gown on the floor beside a blue nightdress covered in vomit. The window is open and I look out and see the neighbours having a barbecue in their garden, drinking wine out of neat, white plastic cups and eating something they're cooking over a fire – I can't make out what. I grab the nightdress, go out of the bathroom and chuck it over the banister to the floor below, to wash later.

When I go back, I look at Mummy lying in the now-lukewarm water streaked yellow with her vomit. I see a hippo wallowing in mud. This is my mother.

'I'm sorry, darling,' she drones. 'I've had a drop too much tonight.'

As if she didn't have a drop too much every night, every week, every month, year in, year out.

'Please help me, Nic, please.'

I could feel the rage building up, slowly, this tsunami of anger, rising, subsiding, rising afresh. I should have stayed where I was, in front of the telly, fingers in my ears, pretending not to hear her. At least my anger was safe there, contained, in no danger of exploding. Most of the time, I had it under control, especially when things were going well at school. Then, I could be a proper little nurse, put my hand on Mummy's hot forehead, make her soup, listen to stories about her former boyfriends (told differently every time) and be the sort of loving daughter she craved. Some evenings, though, I could only be a spiteful daughter, incapable of showing anything other than pent-up rage.

That evening, I reached out to help my mother and took her arm, only to find my fingers tighten around her flabby white skin. I gripped her so hard she winced in pain, and then pinched her suddenly, much harder, until

13

she yelped. I took a deep breath and, as I tried to yank her roughly out of the bath, her arm, weak with misuse, cracked noisily as if it might snap straight off. How I wished it would, this hateful slob of a woman who dared call herself my mother.

I dug my fingers in harder and gave a mighty tug until she slipped and slid around the bath, blowsy body bashing against enamel, unable to struggle to her feet.

'Come on, for God's sake, get out of the bath.'

I bashed her arm against the enamel – once, twice – staring at her arm where my nails had left red marks. She was too drunk to notice. She didn't even flinch.

She started throwing up, the combined effect of my aggression and a recent session with some vodka, and vomit spurted down her ample chest and across her pendulous, neglected bosoms. She was repulsive.

I went to wipe her mouth with a small towel from the rail but found myself almost smothering her instead, forcing my hand over her slack mouth with all the strength I could muster. I screamed out, a spine-chilling yell, which seemed to bounce off the bathroom walls and hang in the air like an echo; a scream of frustration mingled with guilt at what I could have done to her.

'I can't breathe!' she shouted. 'I'm going to choke, Nicola, stop, please stop.'

I was Red Anger, a creature of chaos, a hurricane of hot fury unleashing itself on my weak prey. I could wreak a terrible revenge, unimaginable havoc. I could end her whining once and for all, crush the life out of her, kill the bitch in cold blood – for one reason and one reason only: so she wouldn't be there tomorrow night to call out my name.

'N . . . i . . . c . . . o . . . l . . . a . . . N . . . i . . . c . . . o . . . l . . . a.'

My rage gradually gave way to self-righteousness and disgust. All I could see was Mummy's flesh, bruised and sore from falling over, her damp, tangled hair and stringy bits of cheese and toast floating in the bath beside her, a favourite snack and just about the only non-alcoholic sustenance ever to pass her lips, other than drugs.

I tugged at her arm but she kept slipping away from me, half-sitting, half-lolling in the middle of the bath. I was running out of energy. I flung her arm back inside the bath where it fell into the bathwater beside her. I left the bathroom to go downstairs and make a cup of tea, to try and calm down. By the time I returned, five minutes later, she had managed to stand up, almost, but was swaying dangerously from side to side, bumping every so often against a narrow shelf which ran the length of the bath. Her eyes were closed, her mouth open. I noticed a brown mark, probably diarrhoea running down the back of her left leg. I helped her put her right leg over the side of the bath and edge it gingerly down onto the floor, then the other. She stood, motionless, dripping, upper lip trembling, whether with cold or terror, I couldn't tell. I wrapped a towel around her shivering body, desperate to show some gesture of kindness.

By pushing and pulling her, I managed to guide her from the bathroom to her bedroom where she fell back onto the bed, naked, rolling over, sprawling, hideously out of control. I threw her dressing gown over her and made to leave but she wouldn't let me. She was begging me to fetch the Bible.

'Just get it, Nicola, please.' Her words sounded thick, her mouth dry. 'You know I don't often ask you to do something like this.' This made me madder still. She was always asking me to get the Bible – at least once a week.

'For God's sake, leave it out, will you? Get into bed, now, this minute.'

As she tried to sit up, sighing and sucking her teeth, I rummaged through the drawers inside the scarred pine chest by the door. At last I found the Bible, untouched apart from when the two of us performed this ridiculous ritual and she swore on oath. I took it over to the bed and she grabbed it dramatically, closing her eyes to swear, yet again, that no more alcohol would pass her lips after today, ever.

'I swear on this Bible,' she muttered, with enough false piety to make me cringe, 'I will never touch another drop of alcohol.'

Only a strong voice could carry off such a ridiculous

sentiment and Mummy's was, at this moment, as weak as a kitten's. She didn't really believe what she was saying but was desperate that I should be taken in. She handed me the Bible and then sank back onto her grubby pillows.

'Nic, could you make me some coffee, maybe some cheese on toast? I'm so hungry, please. I won't ask you to do anything else, promise.'

I bit my lip and turned to leave the room. Why couldn't I just be nice? Why couldn't I sit down and chat with her? She was lonely, cooped up in her room all day. It was no life. Before I had time to close the door, she was rasping and gasping, snoring. I went back downstairs and settled into my armchair in front of the telly. I sat staring silently at the screen, tears splattering down my cheeks, yet grateful, in some small way, for the silence.

The following night, I was watching telly again when Mummy started calling.

'Nicola, Nicola.'

I cringed and contemplated turning up the volume but she didn't sound as drunk as usual. It was difficult to tell whether she was drunk or just plain agitated. In some ways, one was as bad as the other, because agitation – even though she might be relatively sober – usually meant she needed more drink.

I ran upstairs. She asked me to get the matches out of

her top drawer, which I did. She liked to have me in her bedroom, helping her, but only when the activity struck her as relatively normal. She'd open her own bottles, hide the empties in some inaccessible places such as on top of her wardrobe, but doing something like lighting a candle was a nice, normal thing for which she could summon me.

I lit a few candles and knelt at her bedside. We did this sometimes, a strange family ritual with only the two of us present. She lay in bed and I knelt on the soft carpet and we sang hymns, really loudly and out of tune. Our favourite was 'Faith of Our Fathers', which we bellowed out from the very pits of our lungs and so it sounded dreadful. The more tuneless the hymn, the more we laughed. Mummy was a convert and, as such, besotted with the Catholic Church. She was one of the few people I have ever met who, sober, actually enjoyed their religion.

Even at eleven, I was well aware that singing Catholic hymns around the bedside was not top of the list of children's entertainment in most homes. For me, however, it was a little slice of happy families, an hour or so of quality time snatched with my mother, usually when my father was away climbing. We never went out with her, to the cinema or to the theatre. We didn't even get to go out for a walk. Her drinking had made her reluctant to leave the house. She would leave to buy drink but that was all; even that stopped eventually and she was forced to order it from the local grocer.

She used to take us out in the car, until we all refused to go anywhere with her. The way she drove was terrifying. She'd sit, staring straight ahead, barely able to see over the steering wheel, never checking the mirrors, oblivious to all other drivers on the road. She was always narrowly escaping accidents. Her excuse was that she had never taken a test. You didn't need to when she learned to drive.

When my father was away, a quasi peace descended over the house and we made our own entertainment. Sometimes the boys and I put on a play for Mummy and spent hours rehearsing and dressing up. She would wait, confined to her room until we were ready to perform. At those times, she laughed and talked a lot, almost daring to emerge as a person, only to cower back down when the lure of sobriety proved too great a threat.

One time, as a teenager, when Daddy was away, I went out one evening and returned to find her standing, drunk, in her nightdress by the gas stove with one ring full on but unlit, and the lighter, also unlit, in her hand. I smelled gas as I came into the hall. God knows how long she had been standing there.

She wasn't always this bad, my mother. My parents moved to a terrace of three-storey Georgian houses in

Murrayfield in 1949. Back then, in a typically Scottish winter, the house and garden were often entombed for several days in heavy snow. At these times, ice frosted the windows, sealed the doors and hung like slender fingers from the surrounding trees. I loved the seasons, observing them all from my leather armchair in the front room. It was like being on guard.

In the sixties, my mother would be upstairs in her den, boozing, while I sat downstairs in my den, and Daddy was away, racing up and down his beloved mountains in Glencoe, 'Munro-bagging', intending to climb all the highest peaks, with his fitter friends. Well, acquaintances really. My father didn't do friends.

My brothers were rarely at home. Long before they reached school age, they were farmed out to various overnight nannies so my parents could go out and have a good time, undisturbed. The minute they could decently be sent away to school, they were despatched to Ampleforth College in Yorkshire, a good school that produced prominent politicians and businessmen. When the boys came home, they either stayed in their rooms or went out. Michael, because he was eight years older than me, enjoyed life in the real world despite what was going on at home. In due course, he became involved in Edinburgh's colourful theatrical scene and put most of his energy into writing and directing. He could always be found at the Traverse Theatre, in its heyday. He knew the Edinburgh scene in a way the rest of us never did.

Peter was more of a home-loving boy, a mother's boy – despite his protests. When Mummy got fed up with me snooping in her drawers and smelling her breath, she'd turn to Peter for solace. Richard had less patience with her – when he was a child, anyway. He was engrossed with his white pet mice, which he kept in a cage; except when they escaped and hid by trying to blend in with the resident mice.

Only when Richard qualified as a doctor did he really take an interest in Mummy's worsening alcoholism. He was appalled when she'd ask him to prescribe sleeping pills and tranquillisers for her. He found it hard to cope with her nagging him, day in, day out, hoping to break his resolve not to write a prescription; he said at times it drove him to drink. She could be so irritating when she'd had a few vodkas and wanted something badly. Rick would be in his small room on the ground floor, through the kitchen and up a flight of stairs, studying for medical exams. Mummy would stand in the kitchen, shouting up at him, her voice loud, edgy and desperate.

'Rick, listen, just this once. I'll never ask again. I promise,' she'd shout.

I could hear her through in the sitting room, even with the TV turned up. She never did it when Daddy was at home.

Because they were away at school so often, the boys had little idea how ill she really was. I think they liked it that way. Peter was more caught up in her demands than the other two and, for that, my father learnt to punish him by singling him out for constant censure.

'Peter's the only one who didn't go to university,' Daddy would say. Or, 'Peter will never make anything of himself.'

It hurt him so much. And it hurt the rest of us because we adored Peter.

When the boys were home, Richard and I often sat in the front room on two battered armchairs drawn up close to the black grate. We used to fight a lot, physically, wrestling on the floor for entertainment, a release of tension. Richard made me laugh so much. When he was home, life was much more bearable. We invented our own language, just so we could talk without the others understanding.

When Daddy was home, he stayed upstairs in his dull bedroom, except when he came down to the sitting room where we were watching rubbishy Westerns. I hated it when he watched telly with us. There was such an atmosphere of tension in the room. I'd keep going out to make cups of tea. At bedtime, I'd approach him as he sat, still watching TV and pucker up to give him a kiss. In a flash, he'd turn his face away, raising one pale cheek in my direction, looking for all the world like somebody out strolling in the countryside, who suddenly discovers he has just stood in a large and messy cowpat.

When the boys were away, I'd stay in the sitting room alone, staring moodily into the gas fire, the false flames keeping me amused for hours. Next to my adopted armchair stood a white marble table where I kept my mug of tea, a permanent friend. I sat hugging my cup, listening to the wind blustering through the garden, stirring the trees as they whispered in the darkness. The house and my chair were my heaven and haven, despite the fact that the house was, quite literally, falling to bits. Slates that had fallen off the roof lay in the back garden, never to be replaced; taps dripped and ceilings peeled.

Everybody had beautifully kept lawns with well-tended flowerbeds – except us. We had a garden full of dead animals, rows of them: dogs, cats, chinchillas, rabbits and pigeons. We treated the animals better than we did ourselves. They were regularly fed with fresh food from the pet shop; my responsibility. They always had cold, fresh water and they were petted practically to death. For Richard and me, the pets were our focus, our raison d'être. When one of them died, I sobbed for days. The animals taught us something about love and death, about grieving and loss. We had a funeral for each animal that passed on; a proper Catholic burial. One of my brothers, copying the monks at their school, would stand over the small body carefully placed in a wooden box (or cardboard if we forgot to go to the shops and beg for wooden ones from the greengrocer). The boys were used to serving at Mass when they were at school. They knew whole sentences in Latin, a knowledge that added kudos and a touch of officialdom to our many funerals. We never laughed during the burials. There wasn't anything to laugh at. We had loved those animals so much and they had loved us back unreservedly.

The neighbours got fed up with us climbing over their garden walls to retrieve balls and lost animals. But they hated the pigeons most of all. Pigeons and Murrayfield didn't mix; unacceptable working-class connotations. My favourite was a proud, dove-grey and black beast with a long neck and sharp green eyes, a homing pigeon called Twinky. Bashful was the second favourite, a brown and white bird who came to a cruel end at the paws of the Manx cat next door. The first time the cat caught Bashful, she broke his wing. From that moment on, my poor pigeon, unable to fly, went everywhere perched on my shoulder. I would have taken him to bed but my mother put her foot down.

I fed the pigeons, watered them and taught them to fly and return home. I nurtured them when they were injured. My pride and joy lay in throwing them up into the air, watching them fly away and waiting, waiting, waiting, sometimes fretting until dawn, until they returned to the shed. They earned me a reputation as a tomboy. I spent most of my time out there in that pigeon hut, preparing my birds for freedom. Whenever I had to go into hospital, Richard took them to Ampleforth and looked after them. The school gave the boys huts for certain pets and Richard cared for the birds between lessons and going to Mass. He said the pigeons kept him sane and I believed him. He hated boarding school, hated being away from us, but then he never really knew how bad things were at home in his absence.

At ten and eleven, he and I spent more time in that musty pigeon hut than anywhere else. The hut stood in the back garden. We had fashioned a trap door at the front where the birds plopped in and out, once we had trained them to come home. I used to hide in the pigeon hut, creep in, close the door and sit on the small wooden stool we kept in one corner, inhaling the smell of hay and pellets. I'd grab one of the birds, hold them with their pink feet pressed up against their bodies like bended knees and bury my nose in the warmth of their feathers. They loved that and crooned for more.

Rick and I were inseparable. The more cut off we became from the world outside our home, the more our dysfunctional bond tied us up in knots. The love we poured into those poor pigeons, for example, must have been stifling, yet, whenever they flew away, they always came back to us and coo-ed at the sight of their makeshift home.

Despite being relatively well-spoken, we stuck out like sore thumbs in Murrayfield. Our house was a tip compared to those of our neighbours, who all had Jaguars or similar and a sprinkler on the lawn. We had expensive cars too, especially my father. Austin was his favourite make. But owning an expensive car wasn't enough for us to fit in. Our neighbours were forced to pretend we weren't there. Next door, we had a knighted gentleman, a charmer with a monocle, who used to watch us from his upstairs window, drink in one hand, typewriter perpetually at the ready. He wrote science fiction and we were, easily, the spookiest thing he'd ever seen. Every time we looked up at the window, a furtive glance or a full-frontal stare, there he was, looking back.

Once, at a time when people still came to the house, a cheeky friend of mine carried a chair outside, plonked it down on the pavement and then sat in it and stared up at him until he lost his temper, chucked down his drink and came racing downstairs to complain to my father, who then turned *his* anger on us. The trouble was that even though the neighbours knew exactly what was going on in our house, my father felt it was important for us to keep up some appearance of being respectable.

When Richard and I were children, my parents still enjoyed going out together. They'd start in the house – he'd open a bottle of wine while she put bowls of crisps and nuts around the living room for all of us to snack on then they'd sit side by side on the settee, laughing and talking, and finally say goodbye to us to go out dancing, leaving us in the care of a neighbour's daughter who always fell asleep on the settee after reading us a story.

But then Mummy started getting drunk while they were out, so much so that Daddy had to carry her home. Sometimes he'd leave her where she was, drive home, pretend he wasn't with her. But then he'd go back because he felt guilty. It wasn't long before his beautiful wife became an embarrassment. By the time I was eight or so, they were restricting their social life to the odd cocktail party until, gradually, over the years, she let the side down at those as well. She'd hand out drinks to all the guests and then sneak off to the pantry, next to the kitchen, where she kept a secret supply. Eventually, she forgot to close the door to the pantry and was seen, standing in a smart party frock, tippling straight from some bottle or other. She invariably ended up in an armchair, dress pulled up to reveal her underwear, legs apart, brain elsewhere.

They had met as medical students at Edinburgh University. Claude, my father, was French. He was fairly conventional and ambitious – a consultant by thirty – but he fell for my mother's ebullience and passion and her total disregard for convention. He had a deep voice and, according to my mother, huge sex appeal.

While discussing a patient's heart, on a ward round, he asked her out and she accepted. In those days, they both drank a lot and liked a good time. Even then, my mother was in the habit of phoning her friends to ask what she'd done the night before. The conversation was always the same: 'Hi, it's me, Monica. I'm fine, and you? Look, I was just wondering . . . you know, last night, well, I'm a bit hazy. How did I get home? I didn't do anything, did I? Anything bad . . . ?'

Sometimes people didn't hold back on their enlightenment but she never apologised. She always said she couldn't bear people who behaved badly and then tried to blame it on booze, yet that was exactly what she did. By most accounts, she was a happy drunk, the sort who slipped quietly to the floor when they'd had enough. One evening, fuelled by bottles of bubbly and in response to a ridiculous bet by one of her fellow students, she asked my father to marry her. He was taken aback at first. They had only been going out together for three months. He told her later he'd accepted because he wanted to humour her, keep her in his bed. Thus it was she got engaged to a man she barely knew. Their fellow students laughed heartily, treated the coming nuptials as a great wheeze, but the couple's respective families were not amused.

'You hardly know the man,' Mummy's mother, Lady Edith De Saumarez Craig, repeatedly told her. 'Marriage isn't a joke, you know, it's not something you do as the result of a bet. It's the rest of your life.'

Her father, Sir Maurice Craig, a prominent psychiatrist, was not happy about the wedding plans either, mainly because he had high hopes for her career and felt she would sacrifice it for children and domesticity.

In my father's home, there weren't any real conversations about the relationship, just strange looks cast across the living room between his mother and father, Grandmère Yvonne and Grandpère David, whenever their son's girlfriend helped herself to another glass of wine. His parents were intelligent and eccentric but very repressed, and certainly not used to women as wild as Monica. My mother detested Grandmère, and vied with her constantly for Claude's attention.

'*Mais, Claude, elle aime boire, ton petite amie,*' was all Yvonne ever said about her future daughter-in-law.

As a family, one of our main problems was a lack of close relatives. Apart from my father's mother, our grandparents all died when we were small children. Despite having fairly advanced Alzheimer's, Grandmère Yvonne would come to look after me when I became disabled and ended up in a wheelchair. She would often take me out at night, pushing my chair miles away from the house. She loved to walk, and always ignored my protests. We'd end up being brought back home by the police: her, dressed in her oldest clothes, holes in her thick, Nora Batty tights, singing *La Traviata* at the top of her voice; me, cringing in my chair, wishing the pavement would swallow us up whole. Nobody did anything to prevent Grandmère looking after me from time to time, right up until the moment she lost it altogether. Her husband, Dr David Thomas Barry, who had been Professor of Physiology at Cork University, was a sweetheart. I vaguely remember sitting on his knee, a short time before he died, watching him play with a train set in the living room.

We had nobody who really cared about us, as well as caring for us, other than Dishy, real name Pearl, our first nanny. Born and brought up in England, she had come to Edinburgh as a relatively young woman – with her husband. When he died, she took to charring in Murrayfield to make enough money to keep her two sons. She visited about five families in our road, yet never discussed them with us, and, as far as we knew, kept our dysfunction to herself. We assumed none of the other families ever did anything odd or bad because Dishy didn't speak about them. If she did let slip some small snippet of gossip, however, such as: 'Mrs Taylor goes to the chiropodist on a Monday,' she would cast her eyes down in shame, blush pillar-box red and change the subject.

Dishy did everything she could to bring us up, but without making it too obvious. When our clothes fell apart, Dishy sewed them. When we hadn't eaten all day, Dishy rustled up a meal before she went home. She didn't really like us calling her Dishy and insisted, even though we had invented the name for her, that it was pronounced and spelt Deachie, which sounded more exotic. You might say Dishy was part of the family except that, at Christmas, she was ordered to stay 'below stairs' with a sherry while we sat in the dining room, clinging onto the tiny shred of respectability we imagined we still possessed.

Dishy arrived on the scene in the fifties and stayed with us until we moved away from Murrayfield in the early seventies. When Dishy wasn't there, we fended for ourselves or had a temporary nanny. We went through nannies as if they were bags of sweets. It wasn't that we were difficult, more that we depended on them for absolutely everything and that was never part of their job description. One or two nannies tried to cash in on our vulnerability – one in particular, a mutton-dressed-as-lamb Glaswegian called Annie who stood no nonsense. She did the cleaning, her husband did the garden, the son did the laundry and the daughter looked after the shopping and cooking. Even though my mother drank non-stop in her bedroom, my father was happy, because, whenever he came home from the hospital, the washing-up was done and a meal was waiting on the table. This went on for a couple of years until he discovered how much money our 'nannies' were syphoning off every week. He ranted. He raved. And Annie and her enterprising family disappeared out of our lives. We went back to normal with a bang: filth, dust, no shopping, the odd meal and lots of yelling and screaming. Dishy was the only one who lasted the course, probably because she only came in about twice a week and didn't stay long enough to see us at our worst.

I used to long for my brothers to come home from school for the holidays. When they did, we retreated into a world of our own, our insurance policy against the mess that surrounded us. We had so many rituals, bizarre things like 'nightlies', when we congregated in the kitchen to eat cornflakes and talk before going to bed. Sometimes, we'd gather at night in the dining room, next door to the kitchen, for the bottle ritual. It's your turn,' Richard would say to me.

'S'not. It's yours.'

'Nope,' he'd say and open one of the bottles of spirit on the sideboard.

One of the boys would taste it.

'She's been at this one, definitely.' Richard or Peter would spit the contents into the sink, just checking to see if Mummy had watered down the bottle after helping herself. Poor Mummy. Nothing she did went unnoticed.

We hardly ever used the dining room. It was bare, hollow, with nothing but a table, a piano, six scratched and scrawny chairs, a few paintings of boats and French windows that opened out onto the back garden.

Every Sunday afternoon, as Alan Freeman was introducing 'Pick of the Pops' on the radio, we assembled in the attic and made up our own Top Ten; an event carried out with meticulous attention by Peter, Richard and me through a voting system, a task which took us most of the afternoon. Michael, who thought our taste was downmarket, preferred classical music.

On days when my mother still went out, we played outside in the back garden. We never really knew where she went. She always said she was going out for lunch to The Beehive with her friend, Matty, a well-spoken woman who wheezed every time she moved. Matty wore a lot of green eye shadow and her eyelashes, thickly coated with mascara, looked like two fat spiders.

The restaurant they frequented was expensive, run in the sixties by a man, a big drinker according to my mother, who succeeded in charming her. She loved spending time with him; she thought he was queer but that she didn't mind because he was great fun. She and her friend would have a good time at first, ordering gin for my mother and brandy doubles for Matty. After a few drinks, they'd be stupefied and want to come home for a sleep. Mummy would take a taxi to Matty's house, drop her off, then return home to sleep off the excess and be awake by the time my father got back from the hospital.

Like the house, our garden was run-down, full of weeds and trampled flowerbeds. At the back, there was a long path of pink gravel, from the house, down the length of the garden to a rickety old door that opened onto a lane running along the terrace. At the bottom was a railway line, where we occasionally managed to escape unnoticed by whichever nanny we had at the time. Our most exciting times were on the bridge over the railway line at the end of the lane where Michael and Peter would stand until a passing train covered them from head to toe in smoke. Richard and I would often sneak down there too.

'Go on, Nic, you go first,' he'd say, looking at me, brown eyes gleaming with excitement, convinced I would refuse. Richard was competitive, loved a challenge.

'Okay, I'll go first.'

I'd climb up onto the wall, above the railway, clutch the railings on the inside for dear life and edge my way slowly across the bridge. We were lucky in that we went down there so rarely, no train ever came along at the same time. If it had, I would have fallen to the tracks below in sheer fright. Occasionally, we ran across the track, even though we knew trains were due. The feeling of getting to the other side, unharmed, was so exhilarating it made the fear bearable.

Peter, my middle brother, was more a people person

than an animal lover. When he came home from school and we children were left to our own devices, he fixated on Edinburgh's waifs and strays, perhaps feeling he could do more for them than he ever could for his mother. Thanks to him, assorted tramps turned up on our doorstep with troubling regularity. I grew quite fond of them, though. He would invite homeless people in off the street and make them snacks. One October day in the late fifties, I came in from the garden to find an old man with a bright red face and tattered clothes, his boots practically welded to his feet, tucking into baked beans on toast at the kitchen table. Peter was – still is – the sort of person that 'problem people' confide in: sensitive, thoughtful, quiet, different from his two brothers in so many respects. My mother played on her middle son's uniqueness, telling him again and again that he was not his father's son but the offspring of an Australian cricketer called Hal, a man she'd had an affair with in the early days of her marriage. We could see, painfully clearly, the effect this had on her second son. Every time she said it, the news devastated him afresh. We never believed it, though, mainly because he and my father were alarmingly similar, physically at least. Emotionally, they were from different planets. My father kept everybody, including his own children, at arm's length. He was disapproving, always scolding, terminally unhappy. Peter was a human being.

We all coped in very different ways with being oddballs. Peter was the most stubborn, especially at mealtimes, when the tension became unbearable. Mummy and Daddy argued about money or drink. She had money, he didn't. She wanted it for drink. He needed it to make an impression. He was a good anaesthetist but he lacked her social cachet. Whenever the tension heightened, Peter would refuse point blank to eat. As young as four, he'd pick at his food and store it in his mouth, refusing to swallow. He'd be told to stand in a corner of the dining room, his cheeks packed with the meat and vegetables he didn't want to eat. Either he swallowed or he stayed in the corner. And he'd stay there for hours sometimes, until one of us managed to retrieve his dinner, out of his mouth, in a serviette, when nobody was looking. As a protest it was very effective. He was a boy of principle who turned into an adult with a strong moral sense.

Michael, on the other hand, always lean and on the go, scoffed his food and seemed curiously unaffected by what went on around him. Ampleforth served him well in that respect. The boys were sent away to public school, the middle-class version of local-authority care. Michael had a very high IQ and used his brain to extract himself from the mire devouring the rest of us.

I loved playing outside with my brothers, but only if their games weren't too rough. A favourite was the one in which we hurled red berries at each other. A high wall circled the garden. At the bottom, near the lane, was a tree, probably a rowan, with glorious bunches of red berries. We knew they were poisonous, which meant we had to try them. I can still remember the bitter taste. I bit one open and lived.

The game consisted of pelting somebody with berries until they were forced to surrender and remove themselves from the wall. Sometimes it hurt, as the boys could be rough, but most of the time we laughed. I excelled at removing my siblings one by one – unless Peter was playing. It was as if he put all his anger into those berry-throwing sessions. He even looked different afterwards, more relaxed, sociable. Although I hurled back berries with all my strength, I was no match for him and always ended up howling, jumping off the wall and running into the house or retiring to my pigeon hut, locking the door for a prolonged sulk.

Sometimes Richard would join me in the hut, say sorry, and we'd stay in there for hours, talking about the pigeons or about Ampleforth and how much he hated it. Richard was one of those children who wanted to be at home, no matter what happened there. If we'd lived down a sewer with rats for parents, he would have wanted to be with us. My mother always said he was afraid he might miss something; one reason why he had rushed out so quickly, as well as early, on the day of his birth.

Richard and I were so similar: intense, living for the moment, worrying about Mummy yet craving distraction from her drinking. We were both slightly mad, always chasing rainbows.

# Chapter 2

# A Price for Everything

We excelled at being odd. Her drinking apart, my mother was way out there, with constant money-making schemes she wanted to put into practice. In the initial stages, before she descended into alcoholic chaos, the money was supposed to fund a lavish lifestyle of champagne and dinner parties as well as nannies to keep us four children out of her hair. Mummy paid for everything – for Ampleforth and for holidays. She had her father's money in trust. The capital was supposed to go to us and the income to my mother, although she was forever trying to get the trustees to release our money to her for drink. She had enough money but felt she needed more. She was always spending yet we didn't have much to show for it. If she wanted something, she bought it. Nevertheless, the furniture still looked bedraggled and our clothes were never anything special. Eventually, after several years of enjoying herself, she began to see that she was going to run out of savings and decided she needed to make money, but couldn't face going back to work.

The chinchillas, a cross between rats and rabbits, were part of that desperation. My mother decided she'd somehow, single-handedly, be able to turn them into handbags. She kept the strange animals in a large cage, in what we called the back kitchen, a dirty, stone-floored room on the way out to the garden. The parents were called Romeo and Juliet and they bred as rapidly as they breathed. What fascinated my brothers about them was that, whenever they approached the cage, the animals would stand up on their hind legs and pee in their faces. The boys sneaked up on them when they weren't looking, endlessly trying to catch them without being peed on, but always failed. We never knew whether this was some sort of greeting in the chinchilla world or a warning to stay away.

I slept in a bedroom with a sloping ceiling, which I painted black because I thought it would make me more interesting. Richard slept a lifetime away; down a flight of squeaking stairs, along a dark, dismal hallway, through the huge, cosy kitchen, up another flight of stairs and in a small room, which, for some unknown reason, we called the attic. At least, he slept there until Mummy decided to breed chickens, and converted his room into a sort of mini farmyard for her babies. Richard's bed and clothes were moved to a cupboard upstairs, just off a landing where we used to play 'murder in the dark'. Mummy was determined to make a fortune from selling chickens' eggs. Everybody needs eggs, she would tell us, and the neighbours can 'bloody well buy their breakfast from us'.

Whenever we went into the attic, we'd be greeted by a sea of yellow baby birds huddled together, their tiny heads thrown back as they squawked for food. Within months, the room smelled like an abattoir. At the time, we thought all kids had mothers who bred chicks in the attic.

In her way, Mummy was an animal lover, just not very PC about it. Another of her wheezes was to breed from Susie and Wong, Tibetan Lion dogs she had rescued from a cat and dog home. With matted hair that looked as if it had been scrunch-dried by experts, the dogs resembled animated floor mops. Susie had a large litter but sat on the pups, killing them all bar two. Wong was unstable, a rescue dog who had been badly treated. He would lie under my mother's bed, refusing to allow anyone near her. Eventually, he had to be put down after biting one of my brothers in the face.

My mother often stood at the kitchen sink, fag in her mouth, holding Susie's bottom under a running tap while squirting it with liquid soap.

'Just cleaning her up a bit,' she'd say, completely ignoring the washing up which lay in the sink beneath.

Considering her medical qualifications, she wasn't a great one for hygiene. To this day, if anyone comes to stay with me, and offers to wash up, I always do it a second time, just to make sure it's really clean.

Chicks and chinchillas came and went, but what remained was Mummy's propensity for selling anything at hand that might raise the money for a case of sherry. We had a lot of antique furniture, but every single piece was eventually badly chipped as a result of my mother falling against it as she stumbled around drunk. My mother tried to sell the antiques for drink money but was never offered more than a few pounds – which she usually took. She'd advertise in the local paper. When anyone came to the house to look at what she was selling, she would show them other items as well: paintings, jewellery, old clothes. People bought them. Her posh voice seduced them into believing they were getting a bargain. Sometimes they were. Things vanished: solid silver tankards, a Dutch still life, a few School of Canaletto paintings. My mother would be overjoyed when she sold a painting, probably worth thousands, for a few pounds.

Our house in Murrayfield was known to most of Edinburgh's antique dealers. They came round when they felt like it: Faganesque characters, gleefully rubbing their gnarled and greedy hands, always encased in black half gloves, at her willingness to part with heirlooms.

'D'you think I should get that painting valued, Nic?' she'd ask, a prelude to a visit from one of her antiques pals. They called her by her first name. One even had a beer whenever he came round. They always left carrying something: an occasional table, a silver-plated quaich, an old mirror, a painting. They'd fight among themselves, whisper, laugh, then one of them would offer an amount. She'd always take it, even if it was way under the antique's true worth. She believed she had a talent for bartering. She'd talk about how nice the dealers were, once they'd scarpered with half the contents of our house.

Not so much rags-to-riches as riches-to-rags. We started out, pre-alcohol, with a beautiful house that was decorative, comfortable and had antiques on every floor. We ended up in a dilapidated, mouse-infested tip – a one-way trip that took us the best part of twenty years.

One time, she put an advert in *The Scotsman* to sell her designer clothes but only told me once the ad had appeared.

'Designer, Mummy, are you kidding?' I exploded when I read it.

And we rolled about laughing. Even she saw the funny side. She did have fashionable clothes, a few designer items even, but they were covered in stains. When Mummy was drunk, she dribbled and drooled. In the old days, when we still went out to restaurants, the boys used to tell her to take her meal and pour it straight down her front and 'cut out the middleman'. She thought it was funny. And it was, most of the time. But when her eyes were half-closed, her quivering mouth hanging open, the hand with the fork shaking like a leaf in a hurricane, then the food just slopped here and there, down her chin, leaving brown stains, it wasn't so funny.

Among her designer clothes were a few twinsets no self-respecting woman would be seen dead in and a couple of worn jackets with matching skirts. Once, when she had advertised a coat for sale, she sold off half the furniture in the house as well, plus one or two priceless family heirlooms. All the dealers had to do was wave a few pounds in her direction and she'd accept. She feared being without her beloved drink. Simple as that. She never stopped to wonder whether her children would mind her selling off the family possessions.

'How much will I bid for the little black number with scrambled egg on the collar?' I taunted. She laughed, but delved into her wardrobe to check if there was anything really worth selling.

The minute the ad appeared, the phone rang. Mummy chatted away for at least five minutes. I listened, amazed at how good her sales technique was. When she wanted something, she knew how to get it. She said goodbye, replaced the receiver, and turned to me, her face flushed with excitement.

'That was a man called Thomas,' she said. 'He wants clothes for his disabled aunt who's too ill to leave the house. So, he's coming round this afternoon to have a look at my stuff.'

I fizzed. 'For God's sake! You can't just let any old body come to the house. A man buying clothes for his house-bound aunt, come on, I don't think so!'

We argued. She begged me to stay. I said I was going out, no matter what happened. But of course I was there when Thomas arrived, too nervous to leave my mother alone until I'd vetted the buyer. He was a charming young man, tall, graceful, well spoken – and a complete and utter fruitcake, as it turned out.

I then went out, to go swimming in the local pool and to get books from the library to lose myself in. I left Thomas and Mummy in the sitting room, discussing his aunt's disability. There was a real ring of truth to what he was saying; the poor dear sounded in a bad way.

Mummy told me the end of the story that night, every single detail, hugging herself with glee at events. She had taken Thomas up to the bedroom where the clothes were all neatly laid out on the bed, leaving him there while she went back downstairs to make a cup of tea. When she returned, rather too quickly, with a likely coat she'd found in the hall on her way to the kettle, Thomas was posing in her black cocktail dress with the special scrambled egg frills. Mummy, with all the subtlety of a brick flying through a window, had clapped her hand over her mouth and laughed out loud, only stopping when Thomas burst into tears.

If she had a quality, it was the ability to make people feel they were superior. That was because she genuinely believed other people were better than her. Thomas poured his heart out while she sat on the bed holding his hand. Never one to hold back, even during life's most embarrassing moments, and God knows she'd had enough of her own, she gave him the fur coat she'd found in the hall and opened up both wardrobe doors.

'Try on anything you want,' she said magnanimously. 'I'll go and make us that cup of tea.'

He was in the house all afternoon, explaining how he couldn't help himself, how he just had this terrible urge to try on women's clothes. He kept apologising, urging Mummy to call the police. He said he'd never been caught in the act before and felt mortified. She told him she wouldn't bother calling the police because they would only want to try on her clothes as well.

'When you walked through that door,' he said, 'I felt like a real monster.'

'I know what you mean,' she had replied. 'I feel like a monster most of the time as well.'

'But you,' Thomas had said, 'you're such a lady.' She told me that bit with real pride, taking her time with the word 'lady'.

'I don't behave like one, though,' Mummy had replied. 'If I were a lady, I wouldn't have pawned the family jewels to pay for drink, would I?'

After that, Thomas visited at least once a week, tried on my mother's clothes, chatted and discussed fashion and heavier topics like gender stereotyping and loneliness. Once he told her, over a cup of afternoon tea, that most people would have gone berserk after discovering a tranny in the house, trying on their clothes in their bedroom, but Mummy had remained totally calm, which made a huge impression on her visitor.

I was baffled by the friendship. Mummy tried to explain that she never felt like drinking when Thomas was around because she knew he was as vulnerable as she was, never a threat. She was able to relax, be herself. It wasn't long before she started going to visit Thomas's disabled aunt as well. Yes, he did have one, but he didn't buy clothes for her. And she was far too well dressed to wear my mother's.

# Chapter 3

# *Worn Out and Wasted*

Even when she was pissed out of her brain, Mummy always had a lit cigarette stuck in her mouth, in bed especially. She puffed away on it during the night, oblivious to any danger. One evening, when it was foggy outside and she wanted a 'fug up', I was sure she was going to set fire to the house with her cigarettes. I went through to the kitchen, filled some bowls with cold water and positioned them around the bed to catch the ash and discarded butts at the moment she fell asleep. She watched me through hooded eyes, smiling faintly, fag poised, ash about to drop.

In the morning, a damp spring day, I was first out of bed. I washed, dressed, had breakfast and went to the surgery for her prescription. She needed more Valium. She always needed more Valium. It helped calm her down. To help her sleep, my mother took sodium amytal, a barbiturate used by some doctors as a truth drug. How I hated those green devils. I always knew when she'd had them because she'd talk incessantly about her childhood, about places in Sussex where she'd grown up, and about how she'd been desperate to know her father but never had the chance because he was always at his practice in Harley Street.

I'd have loved it if she'd talked to me in this way when she was sober, but she didn't, not very often. She was hooked on hiding, concealing herself behind drugs and drink as if the real her was too hideous to expose to the world. She also took moggies – Mogadon, white sleeping pills that are not as strong as sodium amytal – a tranquilliser called Largactil, and Melleril, a major tranquilliser. Her GP gave her prescriptions in the blink of an eye, even though he knew she was mixing them with drink. He knew because I told him. Mummy often took her pills twice when she was pissed. She'd forget she'd taken them the first time.

Sick with worry, I'd make an appointment with her GP, although she changed them as often as she changed her underwear. The minute a doctor questioned her about how many pills she was taking, she'd move to another doctor's list.

I liked Valium as well, the yellow ones, not the blue, which were too strong. I was once in a stupor for a whole day after taking one of her blues. I took them a lot, when things were tense.

If I went to the surgery, I'd stop, on the way home, in what my father called the downmarket end of town, at Sheila Mackay's house for two bottles of vodka. Sheila was a woman who had made an arrangement with Mummy after they had met at an AA meeting and both failed to relinquish the bottle. Sheila was younger, in her thirties, and hadn't yet lost everything. She still had a home, a husband, children and a cleaning job. But the spiral downwards would be quick when it came. You could just tell. My mother had all these things, too, but she also had the means to survive without her husband. Sheila didn't.

When I was ten or thereabouts and Mummy's drinking career hadn't reached its zenith, she would go to Roseburn, not far from Murrayfied, to Harvey's, an upmarket grocery, to buy drink. At first, she'd order a few respectable groceries such as milk, cheese and bread then she'd take a deep breath, steel herself and mutter: 'A bottle of vodka, please,' as if it were as legitimate as a can of baked beans. She tried so hard to sound convincing, making out the vodka had just slipped her mind . . . when, in reality, it was all she had thought about for several hours.

Harvey's knew perfectly well what was going on: they were used to the posh woman from Murrayfield who always needed more booze. She had money, unlike some of their other alkie customers. The only problem was the other regular customers didn't like being in the shop with this woman because she was unsteady on her feet . . . she looked worn out and wasted and slurred her words . . . she sounded upper class but clearly wasn't . . . her black leather bag rattled, at times, with empty bottles . . . nobody else bought vodka as often as she did, in the mornings and afternoons . . . and there was just something not quite right – even if the staff couldn't quite put a finger on it.

My mother found the visits to Harvey's more and more unbearable. She would have sent me, instead, but children weren't allowed to buy drink and the staff wouldn't have served me. She devised a scheme where Sheila, who had no shame, would buy our vodka and give it to me whenever I came round asking for it. For a fee she kept my mother supplied. Sheila had a small, squashed, hardened face and the strangest ears I have ever seen; they had serrated edges, as if a mouse had nibbled hungrily around both lobes.

On one such expedition, I gave Sheila the usual money from my mother. At the time I didn't know she was making a pound on every bottle she sold me, overcharging without any hint of guilt. Those sorts of friends were the only friends my mother had. They were more acquaintances, people who knew an opportunity when they saw one and were willing to be kind to her within reason, to get what they wanted. Most of her decent friends couldn't cope and dumped her. Such as Paula, a French woman who lived in Edinburgh, who was the best. She would arrive at our house, full of life and ebullience. She was so kind to us, always behaved as if nothing was wrong even when trauma waved at her with a large red hankie. Paula was a devout Catholic. Her religion seemed to fuel every fibre of her being. She was a good, good woman.

When I arrived back home with the booze, Mummy was in a state, drinking coffee, jittery, shaking so much the chair moved beneath her.

'Hurry up, you stupid bitch,' she shouted. 'You should be at school by now. You're always late. No wonder your reports are so bad.'

She snatched the bag from me and took the bottles up to her bedroom. Minutes later, she was back out on the landing, a different person, calm, asking me to do something else, school all but forgotten. Could I possibly go and buy her some cheese and a loaf of bread? After a particularly heavy bout, she liked to nibble on toast and lumps of hard cheese. The rest of the time she just ate cereal. She never concerned herself with what I ate and the nannies were intermittent. When Dishy was coming, Mummy put on a bit of an act, going round the house, washing up piles of dirty plates, dusting, cleaning up for the cleaner.

'Nic, I haven't eaten any breakfast. Nip out and get some Cheddar and a nice crusty loaf.' Drink made her selfish. Sober, she wouldn't have asked, drunk she always did.

'I can't, I'm late for school.'

She laughed this off.

'It's okay if you're late for school occasionally. You'll learn more from your mother than any bloody teacher anyway.'

'They're after me because I'm always late, Mummy. One of the teachers says I smell. The other kids laugh at me.'

She stared at me, her gaze could have shattered marble.

'Get out,' she said, 'just get out.'

She couldn't stand any criticism of herself as a mother. It made her angry, probably made her drink even more. She had been lucky. There had been occasions in the past when she would have lost her children, had we not been middle class and able to bypass the very services that might have helped us. Once, when I was seven months old, she'd been drinking one sunny afternoon and left me in my pram in the garden to go inside and sleep it off before my father got home. When she woke up, she couldn't remember where she'd been or where I was – and my father was already home. He ranted, he raged. It was getting dark and he was about to call the police when a neighbour came round to say he'd heard me crying in the garden and he was just checking everything was all right. My father, the personification of charm, said my mother had been ill and a bit distracted but everything was indeed fine. It was all smiles and thank-yous. That was how we dealt with problems in Murrayfield. We didn't need social workers.

When Mummy shouted at me to get out, I knew better than to argue. I left, thankful I didn't have to go shopping after all. I hated wandering around the shops, not because I didn't want to help her but because people always looked at me, wanting to know why I wasn't at school.

She did the shopping after a fashion, by ordering up groceries from Harvey's in Roseburn. She was a good-ish cook when sober, but most of the time she wasn't up to cooking.

My father did the big occasions like the twenty-fifth of December, bawling like a fishwife as he carved up the turkey, his temper getting the better of any lurking Christmas spirit. This would be after he'd dragged us to his hospital, the Western General, to greet the nurses and other consultants who always asked: 'And what did Santa bring you?'

'A toy, socks, an orange, an apple and some chocolate,' it was the same stomach-churning performance year after year, miserable through to the bone, pretending to be delighted when I was fed up with pretending, sick of living on sweets. I wanted fish and chips, something substantial. There was always food around but I always had to heat it up, eat it alone or, even worse, with Daddy. Normally, when you share food, you do so among friends. Sitting with my father was like dining with the enemy, not a pleasant experience. I'd bolt down my meal as fast as my digestive system would allow.

The day she had shouted at me, I stood at the bus stop trying to calm down, breathing in deeply, storing the air in my chest and forgetting to breathe back out. I loved Mummy more than anything but just wanted her to be normal like other kids' mothers, to bake scones, make us meals when we came home and look after us. It seemed easy for my father. That was what made me so angry. I could never understand why he didn't stop her drinking. I understood years later that nobody stops anyone drinking. That's a decision that only comes from within.

The boys always said Daddy should do something, but they said it behind his back. Nobody dared confront him because he had a thing about doing his duty. He thought not leaving my mother, by that I mean not physically moving out of the house, made him a hero, even if he didn't take any real responsibility. People said: 'Poor Claude, look what he has to put up with,' yet he managed to keep out of it, offering me extra pocket money to stay and 'babysit' her while he went climbing. I hated that. I didn't mind him giving me money. It was just the way he seemed to think I wouldn't stay with Mummy without it that I objected to.

The bus arrived. It was packed, mainly with other schoolchildren and people going to work. It was a warm day in September, a condensation-on-dirty-windows day. I could feel myself sweating with bottled-up fury, droplets gathering in the small of my back and just below my hairline. I studied my dress and jacket. I'd been wearing them for three years. They were both torn and the jacket was missing a button. I blushed, sitting there on the bus. I didn't feel like going to school today, I'd rather dig a deep hole in the ground and disappear down it for a few years.

Most of the time, I survived. Even when my brothers weren't there, if I found one of Mummy's bottles of vodka after she'd had too much, I'd chuck half the contents down the sink then re-fill the bottle with tap water. Usually, she was too drunk to notice her supply had been watered down. If she did realise, she beat me on the bare bottom with a belt. It was the only time she ever hit me, and a risk I sometimes took. She didn't do it very hard, but, on top of everything else, it seemed, at times, unforgivable.

That day, I'd only been in class ten minutes when a guidance teacher asked me to accompany her to the boarders' accommodation block for a bath and a change of clothes. She didn't patronise me at all, just said she wanted to make my life a bit easier. I didn't understand what she meant until afterwards, when I felt so much better. The bath was deep and white, the water hot and soapy. She even heated up a vast white towel for me to dry myself and gave me hot chocolate to drink as I soaked. I found it really hard to relax, considering there was nobody banging on the door or begging to be picked up off the floor. But, however bad, that was my comfort zone – I certainly wasn't used to being waited on by an adult, a sober one at that.

Then, dressed in someone else's clean uniform, I followed the teacher to the kitchen where we had fresh wheat toast, strawberry jam and a pot of tea. I munched away without speaking, lost in luxury.

'So, how's Mum?' the teacher asked. Despite her austere, rather middle-aged appearance, she was kindly and well meaning, not at all nosey. I felt like telling her how I spent my evenings, while my father was out swimming or at a meeting, sitting waiting for my mother to cry out and struggling to cart her back to bed, but I was too embarrassed, didn't know where to begin, so I just said: 'Mummy's fine. She wasn't very well yesterday, but she's better today.'

I could see a familiar look pass over my teacher's face, exasperation mixed with pity. She clicked her tongue, picked up her mug of coffee and took a sip. I didn't mind the exasperation, but I hated the pity.

'Don't pity me!' I wanted to shout. 'She's my mother. I do hate her at times but I love her too. When she's sober we have good times together. She's the funniest person I know, a really good mimic, takes off all the teachers, including you. We did go out once, to the zoo and to the cinema as well, when she was sober. The trouble is she's never sober now. There's Daddy of course, but he doesn't bother with me unless he has to. So, I never go anywhere, really.'

I said nothing, sipped my tea and waited for the teacher to give me permission to go back to class. She handed me my old clothes in a rubbish sack to take home for Mummy to wash. High hopes!

There were a few sniggers when I arrived back in class. Everybody was staring. The teacher came over, took me by the hand and led me to sit beside a boy who lived near us. He had often seen Mummy passing by his house, drunk.

'Hi, Smelly,' he said – his favourite nickname for me.

My cheeks were on fire. It was okay when it was just him and me. He would leave me alone on those occasions but the whole class was looking this time. The teacher turned her attention to him, grabbed him by one ear and frogmarched him out of the room. The other children had stopped laughing, suddenly nervous and unsure. Nobody looked at me. All eyes were staring straight ahead. At break, I was so relieved when my best friend, Jo, asked me to go to the playground with her. We stood in a corner, eating a bag of crisps. She always shared her lunch with me. Her mother wrapped every-thing in tinfoil then put it neatly in a plastic box. Jo was prattling on about television and what she'd watched the night before. Telly was relatively unusual in those days. If you had one, you were supposed to be well off. We had two.

'We watched *Blue Peter*,' she said. 'This old woman died and left a filthy house with thirty cats roaming about. The rescue men had to catch them. They were hissing and scratching. It was brilliant. They had their own cat on the show, too, called Jason. He sat completely still throughout the programme and never made a sound, the perfect TV cat, they said. Then we had fish and chips. My sister had her boyfriend round and Daddy and I sat behind him making faces. Daddy's made up his mind he doesn't like the poor boy, so she'll have to find someone else.'

Jo gabbled on. I doubted whether she noticed me sniffing or the tears streaming down my face. I had a talent for being able to cry and carry on a conversation at the same time. My face would remain completely calm while the tears flowed, as if from some invisible tap. I felt the most miserable ever, humiliated, defeated. The earlier bath and change of clothes might as well have never happened. Jo didn't even mention what the boy had said in class. I think she was trying to spare my feelings but I wasn't sure. Maybe she just didn't care.

'I went to bed then came sneaking back down a few hours later,' she squeaked, 'opened the door really fast and they were . . . they were snogging,' she said this last word so grandly, before collapsing into giggles, hand clasped over her mouth.

The bell rang and we finished our juice. As we walked back to the classroom, Jo took my bag of dirty clothes and said, very quietly, 'My mum'll do those for you.'

Luckily for Jo's mother, I didn't go round very often. I had too many responsibilities. But, when I did, I made a point of leaving my life behind. Jo was always inviting me to stay, telling me her family wanted to meet me. I was flattered, though at a loss to understand why – secretly praying she hadn't told them too much. She took my upbringing in her stride, or seemed to. Beneath the calm exterior, I suspected, was disbelief and shock; something about the way she jumped to my side every time she sensed I was ill at ease, as if she thought I couldn't fend for myself. I still had a few remnants of pride left. People didn't have to know my mother spent her days in bed boozing.

One day, I agreed to go to Jo's for supper. The decision

was historic. I couldn't remember ever going anywhere in the evening, other than to wheedle booze out of Sheila Mackay when Mummy had run out. I was excited. I wore my best jeans and a white shirt that I'd kept in a drawer for a year, just in case.

Jo seemed excited too. She was twelve, a bit older than me but we had a lot in common. She kept telling me what we were going to have for the meal: fish pie, chips and peas, followed by home-made bread-and-butter pudding, her favourite. After that, we'd watch cartoons on telly and then I was to sleep in her room. When she came to school, her navy-blue skirt and jacket were always smart, with the collar of her blue shirt turned up at the back to make her look older. Jo was pretty, with a face like a soft, pink peach. You wanted to take it in your hands and suck all the goodness out of it. But Jo wasn't one for public demonstrations of affection. She was warm enough but kept people at arm's length, including me. We got on so well, although Jo never confided very much in me, always preferring to do the listening – and there was plenty for her to take in. Most of the time, our friendship was confined to school, because we didn't have people round to our house. My father didn't like me having friends there, just in case Mummy let the side down.

Jo's family seemed so normal. Her dad was an ophthalmologist, her mum a physiotherapist. She had one brother, a bit younger, and an older sister. The brother, Gregory, was there that evening, being irritating, pulling his sister's hair whenever she wasn't looking and stealing food off her plate. The sister, Emma, had gone out to meet her friends in a health club where they went swimming.

There were so many routines in this house, normal activities that seemed alien to me, and therefore abnormal. They sat around in a circle in the early evening, when Jo's parents got home from work and drank tea. And they talked. They never stopped talking – whereas we never spoke at all at home, only to argue about whether Mummy had been drinking or not; never about current affairs or the cinema or anything normal. At home, the silence filled your ears, a disturbing silence, full of anger and suspicion.

In our house, sitting through mealtimes was hell, the worst experience of all. The only time anyone spoke was when Mummy asked for more wine and the flagon of Daddy's home-made rubbish would be passed up and down the table.

'You've had enough,' he would shout.

'Just one more glass, darling . . .' she'd respond. As for calling him 'darling', never was there such a misnomer. They loathed each other's guts.

Jo's house was different. Her dad helped with her homework.

'That's cheating,' I said and regretted it even before the sentence was out.

'Everybody has help with their homework,' Jo snapped, blushing and pushing her short brown hair out of her eyes, a sign of embarrassment with her.

'I don't,' I retorted, knowing I was pushing my luck. After all, I really didn't want to be sent home. It wasn't fair. Nobody ever helped me.

'Yeah,' Jo said quickly, 'but everyone knows you're a freak.'

We were out of earshot of her parents otherwise I don't think she would have said it. During the silence that followed, I felt the usual tears welling up. Why did I always feel unable to protect myself? What she'd said was true, and freak was really quite a nice way of putting it.

'I'm sorry, Jo. I shouldn't have said anything. It's none of my business. I guess I'm jealous of your family. They're so nice. I wish I had a family like yours.'

There was a shaky peace. Before we ate, Jo took me up to the bedroom to leave my overnight bag. The room was a light blue with matching curtains and bedding. She had her own desk, fitted with a key so she could lock it. She kept a guitar beside her bed. The book-shelf was bulging with scruffy Enid Blyton books and smart, untouched Jane Austen. Jo also had a pine dressing table covered in a white lace cloth on which sat bottles of red and pink nail varnish and a holder for lipsticks. I looked at her, but she wasn't wearing any makeup. She was far too young, I thought, so it must have all been for show. I was seeking solace in bitching silently, condemning the fresh colours on the walls, the twee curtains which matched the bedspread and the clean, expensive sheets and pillowcases. I left my bag on a mattress on the floor next to Jo's bed, took out a white hankie and shoved it up my sleeve. I was always sniffing, so my father said.

As we left her room, she suddenly put her arms round me and gave me a long hug – so out-of-character that it made me hold my breath in alarm.

'You may be a freak,' she said, 'but you're my freak.'

That helped a bit.

Downstairs, Jo's family were already round the table. Her mother was dishing up fish pie that steamed as it hit the white dinner plates. The chips were passed around separately, then the peas. Her father opened a bottle of red wine and, to my astonishment, poured a glass for Jo. It was a large glass. He looked at me, holding the bottle in mid-air and raised his eyebrows.

'No, no, thank you,' the words stumbled out.

'Wise decision,' he replied in his gruff voice, pouring himself a large glass.

'It's so wet outside,' Jo said. Her mother nodded.

'That reminds me, I bought a lovely red mackintosh

this morning,' her mother said.

'Nobody says mackintosh, Mum,' Jo screeched.

'You'll wear it once then you'll want another coat for the summer,' her father said. 'Women!' He turned to me.

'D'you play the guitar, Nicola? No, thought not. I bet your parents wouldn't stand for it. Jo's really good – but the noise! It's like living in a nightclub.'

I kept trying to join in but, each time, found myself stuttering and lost for words. It wasn't that I didn't have opinions, I did. I just wasn't used to airing them. I couldn't remember when I last sat at a table and had a real conversation during a meal. Then it came to me. It had been when my father had tried to make my mother eat her supper out of a saucer on the floor, saying she was too drunk to be at the table and, if she insisted on behaving like an animal, then we would treat her like one. We had to sit there for ages, it seemed like hours. I didn't dare leave. He and I at the table eating cold, half-cooked spaghetti in silence, my mother on the floor, where she had fallen, spooning her bolognaise out of a saucer, until the gin she'd had earlier finally worked its magic and she collapsed forward, head in the sauce. I wanted to scream out, but sat there, winding my legs around the table, praying I would soon be allowed to escape to my den on the landing upstairs, among the sheets and towels in the linen cupboard.

Jo's family only stopped talking to eat or change the

subject. I loved listening to them, wanted to be a part of this precious thing they had, becoming more and more conscious of how much I was missing out on normality. While they discussed Christmas, who would be spending it with whom, I noticed some dust in the corner of the room, not much, but enough, just at the foot of an imposing wooden staircase. I started fidgeting in my seat, looking from Mr to Mrs, from Jo to Gregory. They were so animated. I think they'd forgotten I was there. I slipped out of my seat on to the sanded floor and trotted through to the kitchen. Pushing open the door, I went in, briefly inhaling the fish smells that lingered by the stove.

Beyond the cooker was a small pantry. I opened this door as well. It needed a good shove and then there, in front of me, was an old dustpan and brush, just the job. I took them out into the dining room and over to the dust, diagonally opposite the table.

I couldn't help myself. Cleaning up after people was my thing. There was always dust, always dirty plates to be washed up, always mice and fat on the floor. If I didn't remove it, nobody did. Even in someone else's house, I couldn't leave dirt, pretend it wasn't there because it became a statement about me: a dirty little girl who lived in an unclean house, on the brow of a hill, in one of the richest parts of Murrayfield.

After a few minutes of gathering the dust and

sweeping it into the pan, I became aware of a long silence, an oppressive sort of silence.

'Nicola,' Jo's mother said sharply. 'What the hell are you doing?

# Chapter 4

## Edge of Society

I was eleven on the day that orthopaedic surgeon Jimmy Scott came into my life. I was making a slide in the snow, compacting it for my oldest brother, Michael, to use, testing it, concentrating hard on getting it right – so as to impress him with my skills.

For the umpteenth time, I took a run at my carefully created, smooth, icy path. I kept looking up at the window to see if Michael was watching. No, he wasn't. I was pleased. It gave me more time to prepare. Finally, sure my slide was perfect, I took a deep breath, ran at it, then hurled my upright body forward for maximum impetus only to drop suddenly like a stone. As I landed, there was a loud, distinctive sound, like a crack of lightning; so loud I imagined the people in the next street must have heard it.

My mother came running out. She was wearing a low-cut black cocktail dress, lots of dark make-up and bright red lipstick. Too much. She and my father were having one of their parties that evening, a Sunday. When they were entertaining was the only time they spoke to each other. Keeping up appearances for the sake of their friends forced them together – albeit behaving more like strangers. At that point, Mummy was still sociable. Daddy thought hosting the odd cocktail party might help him get ahead, realising he lacked the confidence to succeed without her.

The fact that I'd fallen over and did not appear to be showing signs of getting up was proving a major inconvenience.

'Nic,' my mother kept saying, 'you have to come inside. You can't just lie here in the road.' She was kneeling on the road beside me, inspecting her stockings for ladders.

'I can't move. I'm stuck,' I mumbled back, surreptitiously sniffing her breath to see whether she'd started the party without the guests.

It's often said that doctors are hopeless with their own. How true it turned out to be that day. My father came out to the street, reluctantly. He was tall, average weight and balding – from birth it seemed. I don't remember him any other way. He was obsessed with being fit and healthy, never more than two pounds overweight. He was distant to the point of being positively chilly, never more than when someone in his immediate circle showed signs of weakness, vulnerability or ill health. He rarely smiled but, when he did, it was like a burst of sunshine, worth waiting for. Born in Paris, he was very French. He loved exotic cheeses and good wines, yet would never do anything as mundane as the weekly shopping. My father did everything well, perfectly if possible. He spoke the King's English, swam a certain number of lengths in a private swimming pool just about every night of his life, climbed mountains but only if they were over a certain number of feet, read science fiction – any fiction, as long as it did not impact in any way on his emotions, an aspect of himself he kept hidden at all costs.

Anaesthesia proved the perfect job for him. It meant he had a lot of responsibility, for life and death, but rarely had to talk to the patient other than to say: 'Just a little prick,' before they became unconscious. Talking was what my father didn't do. You could have been stuck with him in the tiniest prison cell for twenty-five years and still know hardly anything about him. You'd be entertained by his knowledge, laugh at his risqué jokes, be appalled by his temper, impressed by his fitness and endless self-control, gawp at his ability to have one glass of wine a night and two cigarettes – he started rolling his own when the link between smoking and cancer was revealed in the mid-fifties – but you'd still part relative strangers. It was as if he suffered from some sort of emotional anorexia.

I'd had pains in my legs for years, pains my parents always put down to growth. They never once suggested getting my legs checked out. They were doctors. No one could tell them anything they didn't already know.

'You walk like a pigeon,' my father said. 'You'll always walk like a pigeon'.

It amused him to observe me walking, with both feet turned slightly inwards. I spent most of my life trying to fathom him out. One minute he was embarrassed by me, the next almost poking fun. I longed for him to comfort me, tell me I wasn't a total waste of space, wasn't a terminal embarrassment after all, that I wouldn't end up 'just like your mother', one of his favourite sayings. Never did I feel more alone than on that freezing day in the winter of 1961, out there on the icy street, when I discovered I couldn't stand up. It was my first taste of dependence, of the shock of realising I needed someone else in order to function, at the same time knowing there wasn't really anyone there for me, not in any real sense.

'Your father says we're going to have to cancel tonight,' my mother said.

'Oh no, don't do that,' I exclaimed, genuinely appalled at the idea.

She went to call an ambulance; probably so that she wouldn't have to drive me to hospital herself before the guests arrived. Oddly enough, she had been a first-rate medical student, even a practising GP for a while, but she didn't try to examine me or hazard a guess at what was wrong. It was as if my parents didn't have a clue. In the end, they didn't cancel their evening. She played host while he followed me to the hospital then disappeared after checking on my progress.

By the time the ambulance arrived, I was surrounded by well-meaning neighbours. This made me feel quite important because they didn't normally speak to us, considering us rowdy and unkempt and not quite befitting the usual demeanour of the area. But they were kind to me that day, offered advice and kept me warm with blankets and jokes.

I had been looking after a friend's dog for the last few months, a gentle collie with a long pointy snout, called Rufty. He sat at my side, whimpering, as two men lifted me up into the ambulance. Rufty adored me and that made him the exception in our house. My brothers cared but didn't have time for the slowness demanded by disability. I had done everything for Rufty, taken him on walks, given him food, chats, endless love. I waved goodbye to him, praying he would survive without me. One of my brothers took a picture of him and our tabby cat later that same day, both lying on my bed waiting for me to come home and tuck them up in their own baskets.

The crew chatted away as the ambulance wound its way through the city streets. It was to be the first of hundreds of similar journeys, of me going into hospital on my own, suitcase packed, life on hold. Daddy told them he would follow in his car. It's odd. I remember that day, the slide, the fall and the ambulance journey, but I have no recollection of him being at the hospital. Over the years, if he ever did come to visit, he just sat on a chair beside my hospital bed, silent, embarrassed, staring at the floor. Mummy always said she hated him coming to visit me with her and did everything she could to come without him. On days when she was too drunk, nobody came.

The first time I was in a wheelchair was the longest stretch of all. It seemed like years but was more like months. I thought Daddy would help me through the leg operations, make me see a wheelchair wasn't the end of the world, as it seemed at the age of eleven. He never gave me the slightest crumb of comfort. Not one. I was in hospital first, only discharged after weeks in traction with both legs forced to point outwards, thus reducing my tendency to move about like a dishevelled pigeon. I never asked for help from my family. Instead, I became adept, so resourceful, in fact, that I invented ways of putting on my clothes, even my underwear, without having to ask for assistance. Some days, it took hours to get dressed, but I always managed.

If I wanted something from one of the upstairs rooms, I had to find a way of getting it. My favourite means of transport was my backside. I devised a way of manoeuvring myself from the wheelchair onto the bottom step of the huge staircase and then dragging myself up to the next floor. I developed shoulders like coat hangers. I wasn't so hot at hoisting myself out of the wheelchair. Often, at home, I'd end up on the floor, sometimes having failed to secure the brake, other times out of sheer fatigue. If I wasn't on the floor, my mother was.

The Princess Margaret Rose Orthopaedic Hospital became my second Edinburgh home; my first, really. I loved it there, partly because of the other disabled children, partly because of the staff. Whenever I was discharged, I couldn't wait to get back in again. The nurses cared about us so openly. They washed and changed us, hugged us and chatted whenever they could.

That Sunday in late January 1961, I lay in bed, waiting for a surgeon to see my X-rays and decide what to do. Having a medical father meant I was given a room of my own, in those early days anyway, before we fell by the social wayside. I never found out why but, much to my father's irritation, after one of my long stays in the PMR, he was sent a bill for my room. He raged, so much so that I phoned the surgeon myself to ask him if he could sort it out. He did. After that, my father made sure I always had a bed on a public ward, which suited me because I liked looking after the other children; I even had my own nurse's outfit. I had never wanted to be shut away in a private room, anyway.

The door finally opened and a tall man stood there, stock-still. He had dark wavy hair, deep brown eyes and a cheeky smile. He was the personification of charm – so handsome.

'Well, well, what have you been up to?' he said, standing by my bed.

I started to explain about the slide I'd been making for my brother.

'I hope he's paying you for all the work you've done,' he said, adding, 'Jimmy Scott at your service.' He saluted and I was enthralled, in love with him straight away. He was all I thought about for years; night and day. He came with me to the plaster room where a nurse, surrounded by bowls of white, pasty gunge, started to encase my legs in bandages. Mr Scott chattered and laughed. When it was over, he came back to my room. I began to see him as one of those religious apparitions – statues that appear out of the blue and stand by your bed with a halo of white light surrounding them.

'There's some good news and some bad news,' he said, with the same cheeky smile. 'We can operate on your left leg and improve matters there. Unfortunately, we've discovered you have the same problem in your right hip. This condition normally happens in boys, so you're a bit of a rarity, but there's a lot we can do to help.' He paused to see my reaction, surprised that I didn't seem upset. 'It was good that you fell over,' he went on, 'otherwise we may not have discovered the condition so soon, meaning you could have ended up in a wheelchair, permanently. This way, I think we'll be able to put things right.'

After he left, I cried so much that a nurse threatened to call my parents, at least she offered to phone them and I took it as a threat. I don't know what I was crying about. It wasn't my legs. I'd always known something was wrong. I think I was crying because Mr Scott had been so nice. I thought of my parents drinking, imagined Mummy, out of her face, arriving at the hospital in her black dress, falling about, telling me she wished she could have been the one in bed, not me. I stopped crying abruptly.

When my parents came in to visit the following day, they argued.

'I've just spoken to a nurse who says drink might have caused Nicola to be like this,' my father bellowed.

'What d'you mean, drink?' she said.

'You know bloody well what I mean,' he shouted back. 'It's a disease of the hip-bones which needs corrective surgery. They're saying she's got years of hospital and wheelchairs ahead of her.'

They seemed to have forgotten I was there.

'Isn't it hereditary?' my mother asked, going so pale I thought she might pass out.

Daddy said: 'The nurse said it was unlikely to be hereditary since no one else in the family has, or, as far as we know, has ever had it. It'll be because you drank so much when you were pregnant.' He was red in the face, really angry. 'Bloody Foetal Alcohol Syndrome.'

The nurse slipped into the room. 'Yes, but,' she stuttered, 'that's unlikely when both parents are responsible people, professionals like yourselves.'

They all looked at each other.

'We don't always know what causes these things,' the nurse continued calmly. 'What I meant about drink was, well, it does happen. But it's the people who don't know any better we have to worry about.'

At this point, my mother shouted at my father: 'Stop staring at me that way, for God's sake!'

I never really found out why I had the condition. The operations went on for years. The surgeon had to re-set my bones, pinning them into position so my legs turned more out than in. Once the bones had set, the surgeons had to go back in and try to remove the pins. This was not always a successful procedure. I can still set off alarms in airports with the stray bits of metal lurking in my thighs. There were complications as well, little lumps of gristle that pressed against the nerves in my lower back and had to be removed; horrible fatty chunks, the sort you'd find in school stew. Mr Scott let me keep one or two of them in a jar beside my bed to show visitors.

When they weren't operating, they had me in traction for months on end, which meant I was in bed and unable to move. Later on, if I wasn't in a wheelchair, I was on crutches or walking with sticks. I limped. I couldn't walk or run or play games at school. I became a disabled person, inhabiting that strange world in which you imagine, and society reinforces your belief, you're not as good as other people. I was a second-class citizen, a cripple. This was the sixties, well before Political Correctness arrived. This was a time when disabled people knew their place – at the back of every queue going.

The Princess Margaret Rose became my haven. Every day, in the summer, the nurses carted us outside, in beds or wheelchairs, and parked us in a row so we faced the sun coming up from the east – me, Muriel, who had no legs, Pat, who had spina bifida, and so many others. We lay there and watched the able-bodied children on the Hillend Ski Slope opposite. We were so cruel about those poor children, laughed at the idea of them falling over and hurting themselves, all the while secretly wishing we were the ones charging down the hillside on skis. The more mobile among us helped our fellow patients as much as we could. We felt a lot more useful in the PMR than we ever did outside. In hospital, we weren't cripples; only out in society where people held up a mirror, made us look at ourselves with their cold and critical eye, an attitude shared by my own father.

Mr Scott came to see me every single day, often at 8 a.m. before he started work. He always said I was his favourite patient. I wondered how many other little girls he had, lying in hospital beds across the city who brushed their hair and peered anxiously into a mirror before he swept in of a morning to irradiate their lacklustre day. It was always the same routine. He leaned over the bed, tapped you on the nose with a forefinger and insisted on seeing your 'party tricks' – a variety of leg movements that were a constant indicator of mobility. Sometimes he had time for a chat, a joke or story about one of his operations. We loved him, compared notes about what he said or did on a ward round, and argued endlessly about which one of us he liked best.

Mr Scott came to visit me when I went home as well, twice a week. In later years, I used to wonder how he had fitted us all into his day.

My parents had spent a long time discussing whether they wanted me at home.

'Are you sure she wouldn't be better off at the PMR?' my father would say.

'It's not as if we have people round that often,' my

mother replied. 'We do once in a while but not like we used to, and we can get a nurse.'

Eventually, they decided to hire an orthopaedic bed, with a pulley and a cage to keep the blankets from weighing down on my legs, and put it in a room at the back of the house. I had agency nurses. I always had something to do. I read, caught up with schoolwork, drew . . . I loved scrape-a-board, etching onto a black surface.

Much to her ill-disguised irritation, my mother had to start helping me dress, undress, wash and go to the loo. Even though she always prefaced her nursing of me with the deliberate act of stuffing a cigarette in her mouth, the smell of drink, when she approached, hit like a brick against glass. You just don't expect your mother to smell of drink first thing in the morning, not when she's helping you wash your face or use the commode, not when you're only just managing not to scream out in pain every time she tries to lift you.

There was a comic aspect to it, too. She could be so elegant, my mother – such a lady one minute, only to turn into a four-letter fishwife the next, fag between her lips, ash dripping into my lap. Despite the pain in my legs, inflicted by her bungling efforts at caring, we invariably ended up laughing out loud. What a double act.

Something happened to her when I officially became a cripple – my father's expression, not mine. Mummy feared his disgust, blatant and raw as it was, at having a daughter who was disabled. It was enough that he despised his own wife drunk, but that he should be acutely embarrassed because his little girl wasn't physically perfect proved too much for my mother. It made her unspeakably angry, although anger wasn't allowed in our house; at least, not articulated. It stalked the corridors, tore up and down the stairs, but never found expression, not in words anyway. Anger was bottled up exactly in the same way as alcohol. My mother swallowed hers along with a good dollop of humiliation, over and over and over again.

The agency nurses were a strange bunch. One was straight out of a *Carry On . . .* film. She had blonde hair pulled back in a ponytail, her cheeks were scrubbed apple red and she wore far too much make-up. I loathed her. I think the feeling was mutual. I can't remember her name or have deliberately buried it. I will never forget her, though. She bustled about, seemed to be bursting out of her uniform and yet still managed to have an ominous glint in her eye. You didn't mess with this woman. I hated her touching me, washing me and, when I was able to get up, forcing me out of bed and into my clothes. I wanted to manage by myself but she wouldn't let me. In the end, my mother had to ask her to go. I was delighted. The nurse was annoyed, her apple-red cheeks turned a shade of sour-green Granny Smiths for a whole day when she heard the news.

I missed school, missed being with children my own age. When Richard came home, everything was different. I was able to figure in the household at these times. He loved taking me out in the wheelchair. It presented us with so many opportunities for fun. It made him angry when people stared, as they often did, and he became determined to give them something to stare at. We used to sit outside the house, at the pillar box, just where the road began to slope down towards St George's School. When he was sure nobody was looking, he would let go of the chair, push it gently and I'd start to roll down the hill, laughing and screaming, hands poised over the wheels. I believed I could stop myself if the worst ever happened. After a few seconds, which felt more like minutes, Richard would run after me. However much speed I picked up, he always managed to stop the chair, never missed. It was our favourite game.

Mostly, at this stage in our lives, I was stuck in bed and he was away at school. I amused myself, though, excelled at it to the point where I grew to be in love with being alone. It suited my mother as it meant she could stay in her room or go out with her friend, Matty, and leave me in the care of one of the nurses without worrying.

However, my life would change so quickly. One minute, I'd be in bed, unable to move; the next, I would be on crutches or using sticks, able to go wherever I wanted. I had home tutors, a strange bunch of people who existed on a pittance in exchange for a lot of dedication, far more than I ever found in any school.

On my twelfth birthday, my mother held a party. There were a lot of adults drinking wine, a large birthday cake, even a few children playing with toys that had been given to me, so the agency nurse told me. I couldn't see them because I was through in the back bedroom. When Mr Scott came to give me a birthday card, we sat and talked for ten minutes, as usual, then he stood up suddenly, lifted me out of bed and carried me through to where the party was being held. Everybody looked up when we arrived; surprised, guilty that they hadn't thought of bringing me through themselves.

Mr Scott sat down in an armchair with me on his lap. My head was spinning. Being carried by a grown-up was an experience I'd never had before. It was incredible. It made me feel cherished, wanted, a part of something real. I sat there on my surgeon's comfortable lap, glowing. My feelings for him alternated between a childish crush and an aching desire, which lasted right through my childhood, for some sort of parental figure. We both had a piece of birthday cake, lemony with lots of white icing, and Mr Scott drank a cup of coffee. He carried me back to my room, put me to bed and sat down in the nearby chair.

'I'm going to tell you something I don't normally tell my patients,' he said, peering at me over the half-moon glasses he wore when he was 'on duty'. 'When I was a boy, I had exactly the same thing wrong with my hips as you have. The difference between us is that I had a lot of love at home.' It wasn't meant unkindly. He understood me. He had made that very clear.

With that, he stood up, gripped my hand and gave me a look I have never forgotten, not of pity, something nobler than that, then he left without saying another word. I prepared for the evening in the usual way, curled up, with my earphones plugged in, listening to Radio Luxembourg and thinking about Jimmy Scott.

My surgeon was the exception to the rule, however. The man was such a force for good. Mr Scott apart, anyone could come into our house and do what they liked. It was a Mecca for oddballs. Even my first dog, a Labrador puppy called Jet, seemed to have a personality disorder. He clung to the wheelchair, refusing to leave my side apart from going for walks with my father who loathed him, but felt it was his duty to exercise him because his crippled daughter couldn't. Jet used to growl at anyone who dared come near me, which gave me a vague sense of elation. The trouble with Jet was that the minute anyone stroked him, he'd jump all over them, wagging his tail, instantly abandoning the vicious guard-dog act.

Mr Rennie, a pasty-faced joiner who smelled of Marmite, discovered this facet of Jet's character more quickly than most. He worked in our house on and off for several months. I hadn't been home from hospital very long when I discovered him in the back kitchen, building storage cupboards. I wheeled myself to the steps that led down to the back kitchen and sat at the top watching him, Jet by my side growling long and low. Mr Rennie chatted on, about the chinchillas having peed all over him when he arrived and about the wood he was using for the cupboards. He asked about my school, about Jet. It felt good to have someone show so much interest, an adult prepared to donate so much time to a child.

On the second day, Mr Rennie brought cooked sausages for Jet and chocolate for me, wrapped up in a pretty box with a ribbon. He made me tea, and I sat at the top of the steps, drinking it from a mug as he chipped away at his cupboards, telling me about the work he'd done with disabled children. My mother liked him, even asked him to watch me while she went out for the afternoon to drink with Matty.

Mr Rennie must have been about forty. He was balding, fleshy around the chin, thickset yet baby-faced with a soft voice. Most remarkable of all was his charm, his ability to make you feel you were the only thing that mattered. My mother said he was a good worker. When we were left alone, he put Jet outside and closed the back door on him. 'A dog needs to run about,' he said. He came up the four stairs, stood beside me and asked if I had ever seen the chinchillas 'up close'. Before I could answer, he scooped me out of the wheelchair, carried me down the steps and held me, so my face was practically pressed up against the cage. The animals were sleeping, noses quivering, so Mr Rennie just stood, looking into the cage, jangling some loose change in his pocket. At least I thought that was what he was doing.

There was a smell of sweat off him, as well as Marmite, a mild odour, slightly offensive in an unwashed way. He was trembling, leaning into me, holding me against the cage, still jangling his change, more violently than before. I called the chinchillas, trying to tempt them out to see if they would pee on me. I had only ever seen it happen to my brothers. If only they'd do it to me too. Every time Mr Rennie held me against the chinchilla cage, in the pokey back kitchen, I'd pray for the little animals to appear. Eventually, they did. They peed into my face while Mr Rennie squirted stuff – sperm, I later discovered – all over the back of my trousers. I didn't like him doing it, liked it even less when he sponged me down afterwards with cold water from the old sink in the corner. I knew something wasn't right but wasn't sure what to do about it. I didn't dare tell my mother. I'd already incurred her wrath by telling her about the Steely Man who walked past our house with a long mac trailing oddly behind him. He never did anything other than make clucking noises and come too close, touching my arm all the time.

'For God's sake, Nic, I'm not calling the police because a man makes clucking noises at you,' was all she said. 'The poor man, he's probably just trying to be friendly.'

People weren't attuned to child abuse back then in the way they are now. They turned a blind eye, if they acknowledged it at all. I once confided in my father, told him the coalman, who delivered sacks of coal to our neighbours, had exposed himself to me in the back lane while I was out there one morning with Jet. The flesh he showed me was whitish-pink and the rest of his body, the visible bits, were black with coal dust. He did it while standing up on the back of the lorry so the driver wouldn't see him, but I could. My father laughed when I told him, a cruel little laugh and said: 'Nobody's going to be looking at a girl in a wheelchair.'

In a sense my father was right. A wheelchair provides a wonderful shield from the world; a great place in which to hide away. It's just a matter of saying: 'I can't do this' and 'I can't do that. I'm disabled, you see.' But a wheelchair provides the perfect alibi for a would-be abuser. If you want to interfere with a child, where better to choose: a sitting target, a captive audience. Mr Rennie thought so, anyway.

I was upset when I finally understood what had been going on. I'd foolishly imagined he'd sought out my company – which he had, but only so he could press himself up against me over by the cage. He once stuffed his horrid, white, chubby fingers down my pants while I was sitting in the chair at the top of those dark grey stairs. I absolutely froze. Neither of us ever said anything. You don't during moments as bleak as those. I tried asking Mr Rennie to stop lifting me, said it hurt too much. When he ignored me, I said I'd tell my mother but wanted to pluck out my own tongue when I saw what he did next. He opened the back door and called in Jet.

'Watch this,' Mr Rennie said, his quiet voice louder and more aggressive than usual. He took Jet by the collar, held him slightly away from him and started kicking him with his bovver boots; first with his right foot, then his left, twice. Jet yelped. I screamed. If only the dog would turn on him, but he just kept yelping. I had made Mr Rennie very, very angry.

'Please stop, please,' I sobbed. I swear the stabbing pain in my heart would have killed me if he'd gone on kicking Jet. He stopped at exactly the same time as the front door opened and we both heard my mother walk in, put down some bags in the hall then stroll into the kitchen. She had a half-baked smile on her face, one that told me how many gins she'd had with Matty.

'Hi,' she said, too loudly, to Mr Rennie.

'Hello, Mrs Barry,' he said, his voice as soft and carefree as ever. 'Cup of tea?'

Before I could open my mouth, he added: 'Poor little Jet's had a bit of a fright, got caught in the door when I was shutting it. Made a hell of a racket.'

I looked at the man with so much loathing I thought I saw him wince.

'Mummy, Mummy, put Jet on my lap, please,' I shouted.

My mother didn't seem at all perturbed by the request but stood on Jet's paw as she bent, drunkenly, to pick him up. He yelped again. I took that poor darling dog in my arms and cradled his warm body, rubbing one hand the length of his back to check nothing was broken. Not that I would have known. He was whimpering, making a low muttering sound, and shaking. That night I took him to bed with me and he slept curled up in my arms, snoring quietly. I felt really guilty. I loved that dog so much. I looked up Mr Scott's home phone number – he would have known if any of Jet's bones had been damaged – but didn't dare ring. The kicking had been my fault, totally, for opening my big mouth. I didn't deserve a dog as wonderful as Jet.

The next day, when Dishy and I were alone, I told her Mr Rennie gave me the creeps, let slip that I'd seen him kicking Jet but told her she mustn't tell anybody that bit. She went bright red but didn't say anything. Maybe she had sensed something about him. Dishy spoke to my mother that afternoon, in front of me. All she said was if

Mr Rennie didn't go, she would. My father made a phone call and we never saw him again.

# Chapter 5

# Envy and Shame

At thirteen, I wanted to leave home, go anywhere, I didn't care where. One night, when Mummy was wandering about the house, drunk, she came into my bedroom thirty-two times. I know because I counted, watching in silent despair as she jiggled the door handle backwards and forwards, fell into the room and asked where her gin was. Had I seen it? She was maddening.

I had tried asking Jimmy Scott to take me back into hospital, pretending I had pains in my groin where he'd operated before, but the X-rays didn't show anything. I was so disappointed that, realising I had nothing to lose, I decided to risk telling him the truth. When I told him I'd invented pain to get back into hospital, he tried to analyse me rather than judge me, and said he had to talk to my GP, which he did.

My GP was already aware of my desperation because

I had been making repeated trips to his surgery to tell him how bad things were at home. He now went to my father and insisted that I went to boarding school. My father thought it a brilliant idea. He didn't like me being at home – at least, that was the impression I was always left with. This proposal threw me into turmoil. I was scared, somewhat arrogantly, of going, worried about the mess I would be leaving behind. I wanted to go so I might hang onto any shred of sanity I had left, but I feared leaving my mother alone, because leaving her with my father amounted to leaving her alone and I would only, now, be there to care for her during the school holidays. Furthermore, going away meant being parted from Mr Scott! On the other hand, home was unbearable, with fewer and fewer periods of respite from my mother and her drinking. Also, my education had so far been erratic. Most days I tried to go to school but, all too often, Mummy needed me at home.

At the time, I imagined I was the only child in the world begging to be sent away to boarding school. Looking back, I suspect I was one of thousands – begging to go one minute; fearful, yet bizarrely optimistic, the next.

The convent, far away from Edinburgh in Littlehampton, Sussex, contained the usual mix of children you'd find in any day school – clever, thick, well-adjusted, happy, unhappy, horrible and nice. Some, like me, were misfits, plucked from families with serious problems; a few were there because their parents had scrimped and saved, fondly imagining they were giving their little darlings the best opportunities life had to offer. Others, like my best friend, Liz, had parents working abroad.

Our school was all whitewashed walls, red-tiled floor, and long, dark-brown corridors that smelled of vinegary cabbage. The corridors went round pokey bends, their monotony broken by statues of Our Lady dotted here and there, as if we needed reminding this was a Catholic school; it was drummed into us every breathing moment of the day and night. We spent our time on our knees, in confession, at communion, at Mass or praying. We also had to be on our knees to clean, and we did a lot of that. But I wasn't just used to it, I was good at it!

There were about three hundred boarders, each of us a mini expert at dealing with the nuns. We developed a built-in alarm system that involved listening out for the rattling of rosary beads, the sound which alerted us to their flapping veils well before they arrived. Fortunately, the nuns never rumbled our early-warning system.

I was always being punished for talking at night. The punishment involved standing in a heated cupboard, used for drying underwear, for several hours at a time, learning Cicero's letters, this being one of our set books. I learned a lot in that horrible little cupboard, full of dangling bras and pants, drip, drip, dripping onto the floor where I stood. Despite my disability and all that went on at home, I was determined to pass my exams. I wouldn't allow myself to fail.

I picked up an embarrassing habit of genuflecting everywhere because convent life obliged us to do it so often. Years later, when I had to brave the grown-up world outside, I genuflected in the cinema and theatre, everywhere – although, the minute I left school, I became so lapsed as a Catholic that, if I did find myself in a church, I'd start looking round for an ice-cream girl during the sermon.

Our school wasn't cheap. I don't know how it came about but, during my last three years, my parents didn't pay for my education. They told the nuns, in lengthy letters taken to school by me, that they couldn't afford the fees because of my mother's ill health, and begged them to take me for nothing. The implication was that, as they were nuns, they should recognise a charity case when they saw one. Few things embarrassed me – just as well, given my home situation – but this non-payment of fees left me feeling utterly mortified. Everybody knew my father was a consultant. Everybody knew my brothers were at Ampleforth College. The message struck me as horribly clear – they didn't want to pay for me to be educated. My father, who, in any case, didn't believe in educating girls, did exactly the same when I went on to St Andrew's University, years later. He refused to pay, despite what used to be called 'a means test' stating quite clearly that he could afford it.

Not that the convent was high-achieving academically. In fact, educational standards were so low that, if any girl was accepted by Oxford or Cambridge, the whole school was given a day off. In the entire eight years I was there, we only ever had one day off. Mind you, the low expectations suited my slow academic progress. Every time I thought I was getting somewhere with a subject, hospital would beckon. I missed large chunks out of every year. However, the nuns were incredibly flexible and accepted me back whenever I stumbled through the school gates on crutches after an unscheduled spell in the north. They were always telling me what I couldn't do as a disabled child, never what I could. As a result, I excelled in the second-class citizen approach to life. Among my peers, I was always the odd one out. I didn't do gym or run or play hockey, and the nuns stopped me doing maths, geography and history because they thought I had too much on my plate.

When I did have to go to hospital for operations, recuperation sometimes took months and had to be done at home. After I'd successfully battled to persuade my father, my friend Liz was allowed to come and stay with us in Edinburgh a couple of times. Liz was a sophisticated child in many ways. We shared a number of characteristics including a sense of humour that, at times, bordered on hysteria, and a relentless desire to work. She stuck close by my side throughout her visits, confessing she thought our set-up was downright odd, yet we dealt with it in the way we coped with everything, by giggling. This response altered my perception of home for the first time, albeit briefly. For the time she befriended me at school, she lightened the load in the way no drink or drug ever had.

Sometimes I stayed with Liz and her aunt and uncle in Sidcup, Kent. We had so much fun in their house that I used to ask them, periodically, to adopt me. It was their ordinariness I craved; that family who sat together in a circle talking in the evenings or who prolonged dinner by chatting at the dining table, instead of escaping to separate rooms. A psychiatrist once told me I had an Atlas personality, meaning I carried the weight of the world on my shoulders and didn't really know what fun was. For me, having fun meant not having to scoop vomit out of the bath, not being shouted at while I was trying to watch telly or being able to sleep the whole night through without being woken up by my mother falling about the bedroom. I suffered from a work ethic that didn't permit relaxation, not under any circumstances, just in case something happened and my attention was required. I hated going out and loathed being forced to enjoy myself when I didn't know how. I had a permanent eye on the clock.

Staying with Liz induced a state of mind I know now to be enjoyment. But when I chose, maybe once a year, to visit her family instead of going home for the holidays, my mother hit the roof and drank even more to drown her irritation or hurt, I was never sure which. My father just said: 'Okay, that's fine,' so I always asked his permission, not hers. They coped well without me being there. She relied on the phone, one or two AA contacts and her beloved prescriptions.

Once, when Liz and I had returned to school after spending half term in Sidcup, my mother was so annoyed at my not coming home that she travelled down to London, got on a train to Littlehampton and turned up at the school. We were in the middle of an English lesson when one of the nuns came in, followed by my mother. I knew immediately, by the fraught look on her face, what was wrong. Seeing her standing there in my classroom – her hair dishevelled, wild eyes darting this way and that, strain etched in between the lines on her forehead, while my friends looked on in amazement, made my heart thump loudly. The room went quiet, a study in total incomprehension, yet every single person in that room sensed something wasn't right. Some of the girls continued to scribble while others stared at my mother or looked at the teacher for guidance. When she saw me, my mother pointed.

'Please excuse me,' she said to the teacher. 'I must speak to Nicola.'

She turned to me and said in a screechy voice: 'Nic, I've come to get my skirt . . . that one you're wearing. I need it to go away on holiday. I must have that skirt, please, take it off immediately.'

We all stopped breathing at exactly the same time. She might as well have been making her demands with a loaded gun.

I tried reasoning with her; I picked up my crutches and showed them to her.

'Mummy, you know I can't stand up. I can't undress myself. I need help.'

It made no difference. She came closer, until I could see the pinks of her eyes. I wondered whether she had slept recently. I knew what was wrong. She must have stopped drinking for a few days and developed delirium tremens, the DTs. I knew the high-pitched voice and the ridiculous, illogical requests.

'Help her, can't you? Help her get that skirt off,' she was shouting at the other girls, who had started off looking uncomfortable but by now were petrified. The teacher, a middle-aged woman with a saintly expression ruined by sagging jowls, sitting behind my mother, was signing at us to stay seated.

'God knows at one time she could have taken her own skirt off,' my mother shrieked. 'She wasn't always like this, disabled I mean. She used to be a healthy young girl . . . like I am now. You see my parents won't take me away on holiday,' my mother continued. 'So, I have to go myself. They won't buy me a new skirt. They won't even buy me a ticket. All I want is a short holiday but I can't go if Nicola doesn't give me that skirt.'

A girl called Jennifer, showing a maturity the rest of us lacked, worked out that there was only one way to make it all go away. She came over and suggested I remove my skirt. We were about to do so when, outside the door, we could just see the headmistress approaching, accompanied by the school doctor. They came in very quietly, walked over to my mother, took her by the arm and escorted her from the classroom. Oddly, she didn't object, just went with them, almost meekly. She was admitted to a local nursing home where she remained for several days. When I went to see her, one of the nuns came with me. Having a third person present changed the whole dynamic of our relationship. Mummy spoke to me as a mother would to her daughter, asking what sort of a day I'd had. It sounded ridiculous. A couple of times, I noticed her grinning at me, as if she were enjoying the act and I grinned back. The nun observed on the way home how close the two of us were – an irony given the context. Yet we were close, just not mother-and-daughter close.

Mummy went home by train when she had recovered.

She told me nobody came to meet her at the station so she'd had to take a taxi. When I asked whether she'd told Daddy what time she was arriving, she said no. I suggested that might have helped and she laughed. She liked a good wallow, however unwarranted.

Five years after the DTs episode, my mother made her second – and last – visit to the school. It was brave of her to show her face again – and it required enormous courage on my part, too, but I was being given a prize and wanted her there. I waited for her at the front door with one of the nuns who seemed to be perpetually smiling, Sister Carmel. The bell rang dead on the agreed time of 2 p.m. Sister Carmel ran towards the door, turned the large black handle with difficulty and drew it, creaking, towards her. My mother stood on the step, trying to smile but succeeding only in grimacing. She looked nervous, not a good sign. But at least she didn't look drunk.

'We've been expecting you, Mrs Barry,' Sister Carmel said warmly. I kissed my mother on the cheek. She stiffened, knowing my kiss was usually a preliminary to checking her breath. For once, I wasn't sure whether she'd been drinking or not.

'Frances,' Sister Carmel called, beckoning a tall girl with a pointed face and long plaits. 'Could you take Mrs Barry and Nicola over to the big hall? Everyone will be in there by now and Nicola's one of the first to be called, so hurry. She's won the school essay prize,' she prattled on, mainly to herself. 'Mind you, she probably knows where she's going, don't you, Nicola?'

Sister Carmel watched us hurry off down the corridor. I turned back to give her a nod, just in time to see her eyes boring into my mother's disappearing back, the smile completely gone.

A bell rang loudly as we walked into the big hall where most of the girls in the school had assembled. There was such an atmosphere of excitement. Among all the usual figures in black and white, already seated on the stage, were the judges, various worthies from the town, brought in for the occasion. Making our way towards our seats, my mother suddenly dropped her handbag on the floor. I stood looking at it, gaping, as tissues, lipstick, powder compact, wallet and coins fell everywhere. But none of that mattered. Everyone was staring at the quarter bottle of vodka, now shattered into several large chunks of glass, the liquid seeping out over the assembly room floor with its faint smell of musty cellars. They looked at the vodka, then at my mother, and finally at me, alternating between the three in stunned silence: one or two girls laughed nervously.

I wanted to turn away from her and run back to the door, back to the safety of the dormitory, my one thought being to get away. My mother bent over, scooped up everything but the bottle, stuffed her belongings into her bag and strolled on, following Frances who had by now swollen with self-importance, her nose almost as long as her pointed face. I followed, too, at a distance.

All eyes in the hall were fixed on me; yet, whenever I turned to look at anybody, they'd look away. Shifty bastards, I thought. I was swallowing saliva, gulping it down until my throat hurt, my heart racing, eyes stinging, filling with tears. I needed to be like Mummy, pretend nothing was out of the ordinary. She was so good at it. She deserved a prize, not me.

A teacher had, discreetly, I thought, walked off the stage, disappeared and returned with a dustpan and brush and a roll of paper. She cleaned up the shattered glass, without looking at anybody, before returning to the stage. At last Frances led us to our row, not far from the front, pointing out our chairs with a flourish, checking, at the same time, to see how many people were still watching us. Everyone. I sat down on the edge of my seat, frowning, looked up at the stage and the row of worthies.

Mummy was holding a programme, her hands shaking violently. She must have felt dreadful, humiliated, in spite of her cool exterior. Hiding her drinking was important to her, too. She managed to convince herself that people didn't know what they didn't see, which wasn't true in the case of booze. This time everybody knew. It had been painfully obvious when the vodka fell from her bag. I was guilty of complying with her absurd logic by saying nothing that day, refusing to look at her. I could usually tell straight away when she'd been drinking but, that day, I suspected, she'd taken strong tranquillisers and had maybe bought the vodka along to help her face the reception after the prize giving. I knew all the tricks. She was now without her principal means of support and would probably have to leave straight after the ceremony. Everything had to be planned around her next drink, her only means of coping, she thought.

'Nic, sorry dear, I need to go home now,' she would say in her best wheedling voice. 'I've forgotten something. Give my regards to the nuns and to your friends, especially Liz, but . . .' and her voice would tail off.

When my name was called, I felt sick inside, my achievement totally forgotten. Despite holding my head up, the scene with the vodka had transformed me from confident child to insecure, furtive girl, desperate not to be the centre of attention any more. A prize may have been the right reason to have people stare but I was too used to being stared at for the wrong reasons. Somehow I managed to leave my seat and walk towards the stage, gliding to the front of the hall as if under someone else's steam.

'Original style,' the headmistress was saying in a loud, clear voice. She was reading out what the judges had said about my essay. 'Bottomless compassion, wry humour, gets right to the guts of a subject.'

'Bottomless' and 'guts' were all I heard. I could only think of my mother, resenting the fact that she never felt she could turn to me for support, only to the bottle.

Until the vodka moment, negotiating the three stairs had been my primary concern, but I managed them without falling flat on my face. I floated to the centre of the stage where an old man in a dog collar handed me a white envelope and a big crystal bowl with my name inscribed across it under the word 'winner'. As I walked back to my seat, I became aware of the applause to my left and right. I saw Frances, who had ushered us to our seats, waving and cheering, as were all the girls around her who had seen Mummy's bottle smash to the floor.

Then, I saw the figure of my mother. She was still there in her seat where I'd left her, brilliant streaks of gold in her hair, caught by a glimmer of afternoon sun through a nearby window. As I got closer, I saw her eyes were wide open; her cheeks, normally so droopy and sad, were flushed red, her hands clapping with feverish pride.

# Chapter 6

# Road to Despair

I was watching my father grow angry with my mother. He was driving us to the Crichton Royal, her regular psychiatric hospital in Dumfries. She was in the passenger seat, leaning towards him, swaying, barely in control. Persuading her to go back into hospital for treatment had taken several months and all his energy. The build-up to her going in was always the same. She drank more and denied everything; he spied more and usually succeeded in catching her out. It was no life for either of them.

Mummy had sworn she wouldn't drink on the way to the hospital. She didn't. She got tanked up beforehand. Her promises were a guarantee she'd be absolutely legless on whatever occasion you wanted her sober. She sat in the front seat, head lolling to one side, body still swaying dangerously close to the gear-stick. She reeked of drink. The more she lolled, the more my father rammed the gears into place. Sitting in the back, right in the middle, I had a perfect view of them. Even from the back of the car, they looked miserable: him distant, furious, driving as fast as he dared; her, skunk-drunk yet strangely ladylike, a cross between hapless and hopeless. It was a familiar scene.

We journeyed like this for an hour, then Mummy began to stir, look around her. She sat bolt upright, suddenly, miserably sober, before screaming: 'No, no, I won't go!'

'I told you,' she turned to my father. 'I will not go back to that bloody place. Nicola, how could you let him do this?'

My father raised his eyebrows and put his foot down even harder on the accelerator.

While she didn't mind the place itself and the care she received there, she dreaded the needy among her fellow patients. The last time she left to come home, a lesbian nun suffering from manic depression began stalking her. This was to last for years: letters, phone calls – the woman even turned up on the doorstep once and my father had to call the police. My mother attracted people like that. She was understanding and would have made a brilliant doctor had she not been so ill with drugs and drink.

We thought the Crichton did her good, and so did she, but the effects never lasted very long. They tried everything, even Antabuse, a drug that made her vomit if she drank. That worked for as long as she took it. They gave her electroconvulsive therapy, rattling her brain until her head hurt. They invited us, her family, for long talks during which my father said nothing and we got nowhere – other than the staff beginning to realise the problems at home weren't all Mummy's fault.

During these meetings, for some reason, doctors always sided with my father. It was as if they felt they had to support one of their own. One said: 'So, Dr Barry, how long are you prepared to go on putting up with this?'

I had never seen my mother so livid. She challenged the psychiatrist after we had left. He said he'd done it to get some reaction from my father. If that really had been his intention, he failed.

The journey to Dumfries was always hell. Daddy drove us the sixty miles to the hospital while I sat banging my head against the seat. The prelude to the journey, getting her packed and into the car, took an eternity. Once, when I was about eleven, she disappeared just before we were due to leave.

'Mummy, where are you?' I yelled. 'We've got to go. Daddy's already in the car.'

I ran to her bedroom, saw the suitcase on the bed, half-full of things thrown in any old how – nightdress, dressing gown, wash bag, pills galore, green cardigan, dark-stained trousers; her asylum clothes as she called them. There was no sign of her anywhere. I pushed the en suite door to discover it was locked. She never locked this door because there was no one she needed to keep out. Either she was having a fly drink or she had no intention of going to the Crichton.

'Mummy, please, he's already outside.'

'Nicola,' she said.

'Yes?'

'Go away, there's a dear.'

'Please, you've got to go, there's no point in hedging.'

'You're a traitor,' she whined, her tone confirming what I already knew, that she had been drinking. 'You'd do anything for him, nothing for me,' she bawled. 'All you want is for me to die and leave you my money. Then you'll be happy.'

I'd heard this one so many times. She was obsessed with the idea that we were all hanging around waiting for her money. It wasn't just an idle thought. She really believed it and that made me sad.

Just as I was about to give the bathroom door another heave, my father burst into the bedroom, pushed me out the way, inhaled deeply, squared up to the door then smashed against it. The door didn't budge. He nursed his right shoulder then took a few steps back to try again. He was livid.

'She'll come out in a minute,' I muttered.

'Won't,' he retorted.

There was a fumbling sound, a sticky lock moving from one side to the other, and the bathroom door slowly opened, revealing my mother in a smart tweed coat, swaying from side to side, alarm beginning to shine through her otherwise dead eyes. I noticed her eyes seemed to grow less bright with each drinking bout, her skin a little more pale. That day, she had made up her face into a hideous smile; the raised eyebrows drawn in too dark, the thick foundation like orange mud, and with red, red lipstick, painted just above her lip line, giving her the look of a drugged clown.

Still, as she half strode, half edged out of the bathroom, she held her head high, the only sign of her misery being her painted lower lip that jutted out and trembled. She walked slowly, past us, towards the bed. She closed her case, picked it up and went unsteadily out of the room, down the stairs and out to the car.

My father, looking grim, stared straight ahead of him as we left the house, trailing miserably after my unsteady mother, peering furtively up at the neighbours' windows to check no one was watching. Of course they were. They had nothing better to do. If my father hadn't been there, I'd have given them two fingers.

He worried, perhaps understandably, about what they thought. I was past caring what the neighbours thought. Easy for me – I didn't have an important job. I was aware of their disapproval, the way they either frowned at me when they passed in the street or smiled when they thought everything was okay, in other words, if they thought she wasn't drinking. They knew because they judged her by how she looked, steady or unsteady. In her later years, when they didn't see her at all, they were happy and smiled at us all the time. Ironic because, in those later years when she wasn't out and about, she was at her very worst and she was slowly drinking herself to death in her bedroom.

I couldn't understand her. She'd known for days we were taking her back to the Crichton. It was as if she needed an excuse to blow a fuse. I avoided her gaze by looking out the window, but out of the corner of my eye I saw her wrestling with something in the front. Then, to my horror, she opened her door and tried to throw herself out onto the busy trunk road. She had decided that being splattered across the road at seventy miles per hour was preferable to another stay at the Crichton. But, as the door flew open, it occurred to her she was still strapped into her seat and couldn't move.

I put my arms around her neck and screamed really loudly, a big mistake. My father turned round and roared at me to 'shut the fuck up'. He had seen what she had tried to do and was, as usual, unable to cope. Shouting at me was a way of venting feelings he didn't understand. The car swerved, narrowly missing an overtaking lorry.

Beside himself, my father pulled over two lanes before shuddering to a halt on the hard shoulder. He flung open his door, jumped out without looking to see if it was safe, then stormed round to my mother's side. She was crying, I was crying. My father was bellowing. Cars, lorries, motorbikes zipped past us, drivers peering out, enjoying this brief snapshot of our horrible little lives.

'You nearly bloody killed us,' my father bawled, as he grabbed my mother's shoulders and shook them hard. 'What are you playing at, you lunatic? My God, you're going to the right place, I can tell you. Nicola, get out of the car, please.'

I pushed my door open and made to climb out. He went mad all over again.

'You idiot!' he roared, most of his words lost in the hum of passing traffic. 'This is a busy road. You don't just jump out into the middle of a road.'

I resisted the urge to shout, 'Why not? You just did.' Instead I slunk back into my seat and stared at the back of my mother's sobbing head. I wanted to hold her, at least try to reassure her that what we were doing was for her benefit. I really believed it was.

'I'm fine here. I want to stay with Mummy. I don't want to get out of the car.'

My mother leaned over the gear-stick, fumbled around for the car key and yanked it out of the ignition. She closed her own door then clicked the key and all the doors snapped. Now we were locked in and my father was outside on the grass verge. When he realised what she'd done, his face went from red to white to purple as if he were having some kind of seizure. Mummy, still slightly drunk, was laughing her head off. I prayed she wouldn't start the car and drive away.

Daddy was standing on the grass verge, frowning and looking away from us. He reached into his jacket pocket, the grey corduroy one with the awful leather patches on the sleeves, and took out his cigarette papers. Mummy was still laughing, lolling about at the front of the car, clearly delighted at his predicament. I thought I saw tears run down his face. That was all it took. I fiddled with the car door until I heard the catch release. Mummy heard it too and turned to accuse me, yet again, of being a traitor. I opened my door and jumped out. My father was amazed. With them it was all about sides. His and hers.

'Nicola, darling,' he said, putting his arms around me. I think he actually meant the 'darling' this time, something to do with his tone of muffled relief. We stood there on the hard shoulder, looking at Mummy. She had stopped laughing, lost once again in her own wretched little world, lost and alone and wretched. She said nothing when we got back into the car and prepared to drive away.

*

The house was so quiet when she was in the 'asylum'. The Crichton was a private nursing home-cum-hospital but we preferred to call it an 'asylum'. Turning it into a joke was a way of distancing ourselves from its reality, of making it less scary. Now, it was just my father and I at home. He was there all the time when she went away. He didn't take his usual weekends of climbing in Glencoe, said he needed to look after me. But it was really the other way around.

I was lucky enough not to be in a wheelchair when alone with him, to be relatively mobile, in fact. God knows what would have happened if I'd had to depend on him. He was such a cold fish, especially if you happened to be ill. Nevertheless, he was so different when she wasn't there. He came out of his shell, shed his load of anger and became almost pleasant. They seemed to wind each other up all the time. My mother said she drank because of his temper and he claimed his temper was a result of her drinking.

I was eleven when I started helping myself to my mother's Valium. The minute I knew my father was on his way home from the hospital, I'd grab one from the small bottle I kept beside my bed for emergencies. I think Mummy would rather I drank than took her precious tranquillisers, but I didn't care.

My first taste of alcohol came at school, just before my French oral exam. I was sixteen. I asked one of the day

115

girls to go out and buy me a quarter bottle of vodka. She was a friend, and could have been expelled for doing it, but nerves were getting the better of me, as well as a streak of perfectionism, and I could be very persuasive. I had to do well in the oral exam. After all, I was half French. I'd seen my mother repeatedly drown her terror with gin. I would do the same with vodka. I drank a large part of the small bottle, enough to make me feel very confident for an hour or two and sick to my stomach a while later.

I got full marks for the exam, though, and, unfortunately, the experience set a precedent. I could meet my own high expectations only if I had a drink first, just like my mother. It was a success of sorts, better than bottling out through fear. I was afraid I'd be unable to perform sober. That was my problem. In fact I rarely gave myself a chance to try anything 'straight' and felt more at ease with the drunk version of myself.

At home, when Mummy was there, I was frightened of my father's temper, which ripped through the house within minutes of his arrival. He was all banging doors, ranting and raving about the mess and about the lack of dinner. When he went away, he left strict instructions about how much wine my mother was to be given: three glasses a day, not a drop more. She would barter with me to get them all in the morning and then drink her own supply the rest of the day.

Even though Daddy came home after work, it was as if he were away. Once his temper had died down, he'd disappear into his room, shut the door and we wouldn't see him again until he locked the front door, muttered goodnight and returned to his room.

When Mummy was at the Crichton, I once or twice dared ask him if I could sit with him in his room. He said yes, reluctantly, and I sat, hardly moving for fear of annoying him, inhaling the dust that lined the picture frames on the walls and layered his science fiction collection. Clumps of dust hung from the ceiling, a spider dangled precariously off one cobweb, swinging backwards and forwards like a child in a playground. Sometimes we sat at the small piano he kept in his room and he tried to teach me to play, staying incredibly patient as my nervous fingers fumbled and tumbled over the keys.

I had to fight for his attention. But when my mother was at home his attention wasn't worth having. He was cold and cynical, prickly like a hedgehog. He could be brutal in the things he said. When she wasn't there, we didn't exactly make conversation but we did at least communicate, and he was capable of saying 'Yes, please' or 'No, thanks' if I offered him a cup of tea. It was a big improvement on the temper.

My father didn't do small talk. He didn't have any close friends and so wasn't practised in the art of conversation.

Since I had grown up with silence, we made an excellent double act. As a family, we normally sat in separate rooms, him reading in his room upstairs, her pissed out of her brain in hers, me downstairs. As the years passed us all by, they barely spoke. According to her, they stopped having sex a while after I was born, although my father did sleep with her a few times after that. When I was about eight, she sat me down on the settee in the front room and told me, in as much detail as she could, about how he had come into her room during the night and demanded intercourse, and how fantastic it had been. She started sobbing, asking me why he wouldn't sleep with her every night. Was she so revolting? I tried to comfort her but, as I did, the doors started slamming and my father stomped about in the hall. She spoke so loudly when she was drunk, I am sure he had overheard every word. He didn't speak to me for weeks after that, not even to shout, mortified that I knew about his sex life or the lack of it.

When she went away to the Crichton for a month or two at a time, my father even looked different: his brow smooth and relaxed. He smiled when I kissed him goodnight, didn't turn his cheek away as abruptly as usual, all bonuses when you're watching and assessing every move, to check your father really does love you. I used to wonder if he had a girlfriend. Often, when I came into his room, he'd be on the phone. He'd say really quickly: 'Right, I have to go now,' and replace the receiver. If the phone rang while we were both in the room, he'd snatch it and say after a few seconds: 'Think you must have the wrong number.'

I wondered what she was like. She'd be younger than Mummy. Early thirties, slim probably, blonde hair, or maybe brunette, long red fingernails, good at ironing shirts. Things like that were important to him as he wasn't domestically inclined, apart from throwing together delicious meat cassoulets, a French dish with beans, which he kept for days because they tasted better with every re-heating. I bet his girlfriend never touched a drop of alcohol, either.

And yet I never really believed he had a girlfriend. The coldness precluded it. He never showed Mummy any affection so how could he possibly conjure it up for someone else? I remember once trying to take a photo of the two of them, making them stand together. In the photo, she was struggling to smile and he had turned away from her, as if posing for a different camera.

Sometimes I worried about what people thought of us, especially the other kids at school. Mostly, I didn't care. If my mother fell flat on her face in the street and people stared, let them. I'd just help her up and carry on as normal. She was my mother, and I loved her to bits, at least when she wasn't making me so angry I wanted to kill her. The older and odder I became, the less I cared about what people thought.

I always felt guilty about liking Daddy when he and I were alone, because I knew he was so rotten to her. I wouldn't go so far as to say I loved him. In later years, I despised him, blamed him for having deprived me of any hint of self-confidence. He made me feel as if I was always out of step, not acceptable on any level. My belief in myself was based on his words, on him calling me a crippled idiot. He referred to me that way in conversation with my mother, always just loud enough for me to hear. Nothing, not even Mr Rennie and his abusive ways, ever made me feel as bad as my father's tongue, and the mud stuck. I inherited that critical voice of his, used it to beat myself for years, never managed to erase it, not even when he died. But, he was my father. As long as I wasn't in a wheelchair or on crutches, my disability somehow reflecting on his status as a doctor, we got on well enough. But he hated having a disabled daughter.

My father amused himself by keeping wine-making equipment and bottles in the loft, which he reached by pulling open a trap door in a small back bedroom and using a Ramsay ladder. He would then feed his home-made drink to my mother, becoming angry and disgusted when she demanded more. Once the wine had fermented, he bottled it, taking the new bottles and putting them in a small, smelly cupboard. It was a pokey cupboard, a den really, where he also kept medical equipment for work as well as gardening stuff and a toolbox.

In the loft, he kept plastic hosing for siphoning off wine into large flagons. Since this process often involved waiting, he kept a dartboard up there as well as a small air pistol. I once went up there and found a photo of Mummy, an old one, attached to the board; he'd been using it for target practice. In the picture, Mummy was looking young and sexy in a low-cut gown.

One day when he was actually in a good mood, he told me how he'd been up in the loft, siphoning off some red into bottles, when something made him sit up in a panic. It took a while to register what it was: the plastic tubing was lying on the floor instead of wound round two hooks on the wall next to the flagons. He couldn't believe he'd left it like that. Once germs had got into the new wine, no matter what stage of fermentation it was at, the rest of the supply could easily become polluted too. Only when he stooped to pick up the tubing did he see the bright red lipstick smeared around the mouth-piece at the opening. The colour was unmistakable. The discovery horrified him. She'd been up there, in his secret hideaway.

While she was away in hospital, he never went anywhere near the loft; yet, within hours of her coming home, he'd be up there again, bringing wine down the stairs and leaving it lying around in the way a dealer might give heroin to a drug addict. I didn't know then that this often happens in alcoholic families, where the partner and children are used to functioning without the drunk person and find it impossible to adapt to them sober, should they try to fulfil some useful role in the household.

When my mother went to hospital, he and I had our well-worn patterns of behaviour. The first time she was carted off in an ambulance, I must have been eight or nine, I sobbed for all of five minutes and then realised I could do whatever I liked for a month or so. Instead of playing with my doll's house and shifting my smartly dressed, teetotal dolls from one room to another or sitting them at their tiny Formica table for their meals, I could be a real mother – to my father. That was why I made him cups of tea, discarding the chipped blue-and-white striped cups from Woolworths that we normally used in favour of the posh Wedgwood china my mother kept in a separate cupboard. I gave him little cakes on proper side plates. I washed up afterwards, so carefully, rinsing every plate, rejoicing in the temporary cleanliness that surrounded us.

Very occasionally, he let me miss school so I could do the shopping. He didn't like it when I missed school to look after Mummy, said I'd lose out later on when kids of my own age would be ahead of me. When I was doing the shopping for him, however, it was different. I'd put on my mother's pinny as soon as I got up in the morning, make my bed, tidy up downstairs and listen to Cliff Richard records while he sat reading science fiction in the sitting room. I did most of these things when she was around as well, but then it was a duty. On my own, without her butting in with requests and prompts all the time, I enjoyed it. It made me feel important, as if I mattered after all.

One evening, when we had settled in his room after some rather good mince and tatties, a meal prepared and cleared away by me, the phone interrupted the silence like some violent intruder. I waited for Daddy to say: 'Wrong number,' but, instead, he kept saying, 'Yes, okay, that'll be fine.' He put down the receiver, sighed, said he was going to get a drink. While he was out of the room, fumbling in his drinks cupboard, I could hear him cursing loudly under his breath. He returned with a tumbler full of whisky.

'Your mother's back tomorrow,' he said flatly.

The subject of Mummy and her inevitable return had been taboo up until now. There had been an atmosphere these last few weeks. It was as if she'd died but neither of us could come out and say it had actually been for the best, so we were pretending it hadn't happened at all. He and I had grown closer. I felt as if I knew him better, even if I didn't particularly like what I had discovered. He really was cold and remote, a poor soul in so many ways. He had been in love with Mummy and he felt so let down. Now she was coming back. That was that. My mood changed, sadness crept in through the cracks in my armour. I felt myself slipping back into my former life, back to living in the shadow of the bottle, a time when days passed by like leaden soldiers.

I was surprised at how angry I felt about her coming back home so soon. I'd worked hard to keep the house clean and had written screeds to my brothers telling them how mouse-free the house was. Now, out of the blue, she was going to spoil everything. I had no understanding or compassion for her at that stage in my life. That only came later with my own experience of alcoholism. The poor woman couldn't do anything right, literally. We prevented her from getting better.

Back then, when she came home from hospital, I resigned myself to dirt and mice, to being hungry, to shouting and screaming. It's what the Barrys did. I began preparing for her return immediately, making up her bed with sheets that, as usual, were stained but clean. Everything was stained in our house: towels, sheets, blankets. There were yellow and brown stains, red ones, a few green and purple – medicines of various kinds. My father used to say, unkindly, that Mummy was 'like a baby', a 'mass of uncontrolled apertures'. He was never nice about her. Mind you, she savaged him behind his back most of the time, too, saying he was a cold potato, bad tempered and cruel, but, 'Listen, dear,' she'd add, 'he is a good father.' They both seemed to think that being a good father meant not leaving. As long as he was there in the house, however distant and useless, he was doing his duty.

Once her bed was ready, I set about locking up Daddy's drinks cupboard. It was the first thing you saw when you came into the house. I kept reminding him that the cupboard was open, until he said he'd lost the key. I knew he was lying because I found it in his hiding place, behind the small alarm clock in his bedroom. It freaked me out. It was the weirdest thing I had ever known him do.

Usually, when she came home, it was two or three days before she helped herself to his drink, and then only after he'd exploded because she'd failed to do something properly. This time she started drinking again because of a row over a dirty saucepan. He had picked up a small saucepan, held it up to the light and inspected it, turning up his nose at some piece of congealed food.

'What do you mean, "Clean it properly"?' my mother had asked him, assertively sober for a change.

'I mean *properly*, with washing-up liquid and hot water, like Nicola does,' he bawled back. 'No, wait, I'll show you what I mean.' And he opened all the cupboards, grabbed as many saucepans as he could find and hurled them on the floor, splitting some of the tiles. The banging and crashing was scary. The phone rang before he could progress to the rest of the kitchen utensils. My mother had a drink that afternoon.

I hated him at times like that. It was as if he wanted her to drink. Instead of telling him how I felt, instead of making my anger plain, I made him cups of tea and fetched and carried until he told me I was his 'little princess'. That made me happy. I needed to be somebody's princess, even if it was only his.

On the morning of her return, I scrubbed out the kitchen and tried to make an apple crumble. My friend Jo's mother had shown me how when I'd stayed at her house. Mummy appeared suddenly by taxi and strolled through the door as cool as a cucumber. I suppose I thought she might look nervous or pleased to be back but she was neither. She was uncharacteristically confident, and it was my father who looked uneasy. We weren't used to seeing her sober, upright and talking without slurring her words. It was like having a total stranger in the house. Each time she went off to the Crichton, she was that bit worse, drunker than the time before. Consequently, the change in her when she came back was ever more dramatic.

She asked me to make her a cup of tea. I went out to the kitchen and cut her a slice of burnt apple crumble.

'Strong, Nicola,' she called. She was wearing a new suit, quite smart, navy jacket and skirt. She'd lost a lot of weight, her blowsy cheeks had narrowed; her eyes were clear. For the first time I could actually see what a lovely shade of brown they were, with her long, dark lashes that swept up and down like mini paint-brushes. She looked fantastic. Even my father sat with his mouth open, gaping, as if he were being shown exactly what he had lost. And he had lost her. We all knew that. Sure, she was there with us, but only physically. When her mind wasn't in the bottle, who knows where it went, not to us, that was for sure.

'I thought we'd have a real roast dinner tonight,' she said with new, sober confidence, 'a proper Sunday roast.'

Daddy and I looked at each other. His mouth snapped shut and he tried to stop gaping. Who was this person? I knew that was what he was thinking. How dare she breeze into our house and start telling us what we were going to eat? Bugger her. She's had enough chances to cook and clean for us but all she'd done was lie around, pissed out of her bloody skull. I know Daddy swore in his thoughts, so I did too. I could see new lines on his face, his brow already etched with fury. This anger was the strangest emotion I have ever experienced. I never attempted to discuss it with anybody. At its heart the anger seemed to say: 'We don't want you drunk, but we don't want you sober, either.' We punished my poor mother by sending her away to dry out and we punished her for coming back a different, more capable person, which was what we thought we had wanted in the first place.

'I bought a joint of beef on the way back here,' she said. 'I asked my friend to stop at the supermarket.' She laughed, in her old sexy way, a growl from the belly. I smiled straight at her. God, for one split second I might actually have made her feel welcome. She was trying too damned hard, and we were blocking her at every turn, yet none of us knew why. I stood up.

'I'll put the meat in the oven,' I said, too loudly. 'I got some vegetables yesterday, potatoes as well. Yummy. We can have roast potatoes.' I didn't have a clue how to make a Sunday roast but I was determined not to let her do it. No way. This was rapidly turning into a competition.

All of a sudden, it was as if the heavens had opened. My mother leapt to her feet, radiant smile gone; standing there in her navy suit, drawing in breath and letting it out again with a rasp that shook the whole room. My father clutched the arms of his chair, his knuckles whitening.

'*I* will cook the meal!' she roared, mainly for my benefit. '*I* will lay the table, and we will eat together *as a family*. D'you hear?'

I sat down again, stared at the floor, tears threatening; tears I was determined she shouldn't see. Then I jumped out of my armchair, grabbed my rucksack off the settee and headed for the door.

'Well, don't do any for me!' I shouted, slamming the door so loudly the noise seemed to echo down the street as I hurried away, an insolent child with hot saltwater drops rolling down her stubborn little face.

# Chapter 7

# *Stolen Moments*

It wasn't just my mother who went away to recuperate. When my father went off climbing he'd often give me money to look after Mummy in his absence. He'd go whenever he could get time off work, usually once a month for a whole weekend.

One Christmas, just before he left for Chamonix with Richard, Daddy gave me a brilliant new blue bike and a pair of boots with a small heel. I was ten. I remember him wincing when I said: 'Hey, you should go away more often.' He felt guilty – because he couldn't cope with what was going on in the house. He slipped me a fiver, a lot of money in 1960, hush money. He'd sometimes whisper: 'Sorry,' as he disappeared down the stairs in the way of a robber fleeing the scene. He'd say such things as: 'It's not as if I'm leaving you on your own,' knowing damn well that's exactly what he was doing. 'Your mother'll be fine.' And off he would go. In a sense, it didn't make any difference when he wasn't there. She'd be legless, exactly the same as every other day. It was just that I worried something might happen. Even though I was used to things happening.

Yet Mummy and I were both so relieved when he left. We'd literally breathe out, long and hard, as he slammed the door behind him. When my father was away, my mother would either be very relaxed and chatty or go on an out-and-out bender, sending me up to the loft, among all the spiders, to siphon off some of his home-made wine. Things did go wrong when Daddy was away but I usually managed to deal with them. The scariest times were when she came into my bedroom in the middle of the night, drunk, stumbling about in the dark. On one of these nights, she fell on top of me and lay there, refusing to move, a ton weight. I felt all the air being squeezed out of my chest as she crushed me into the mattress. I shoved and kicked but she wouldn't budge. I was really frightened. It had happened before but not with me beneath her. This was just before the condition in my legs was diagnosed and my limbs ached. They felt as if they'd break in two. I managed to drag myself over to the edge of the bed so that I could breathe without too much discomfort.

When the boys came home, which they only ever did in their school holidays, Michael, the eldest, was technically in charge and shouted at the rest of us when we whispered during the night. He was eight years older than me, a gawky teenager, sociable, clever and mortified by us, his family. Once when Mike was staying, he was sleeping in the room next to my mother's bedroom. He must have been about fourteen at the time. I was seven. Mike came out of his room to go to the bathroom one night, saw Mummy's door was wide open and looked in, only to see her sitting naked on a pot. When he told me the next day, I could see the revulsion in his eyes. The sight had horrified him, made him sick.

Yet she often sat like that, staying like it for hours. She was afraid of going to the bathroom during the night, in case she fell or made a noise and disturbed my father, so she said. But she would take her sleeping pills first, drink some vodka then decide she had to pee before sleeping. Somehow she'd engineer herself onto the pot and fall asleep there, balancing like a Buddha, mouth dangling open, until, eventually, something would startle her and she'd jump, sending the pot and its contents flying all over the carpet. Nobody ever cleaned the carpet. I used to scrub it occasionally but, after a while, there didn't seem to be much point. She spilled medicine and booze and pee onto that carpet every single day of her life.

My father was almost always at home when the boys were there. He enjoyed them because they were healthy and didn't show him up in the way my mother and I always did. My parents didn't fight as much when the boys were at home. My mother, in particular, loved to have Peter around for chats. Because he wasn't there very often, he had more patience than I did.

The fights were terrible, mainly over drink. Usually, they began at the table. We'd be sitting, trying to have an evening meal – a cassoulet, if he'd made it; packets of mashed potato and frozen vegetables, if she had. The flagon of red wine would sit in the middle of the table.

'Can I have a glass?' she'd say, already pissed from her own supply. 'Nic, ask your father if I'm allowed a glass of wine.'

I would look at her, then at him, then back at her.

'You look as if you've had enough already,' my father would reply.

'For God's sake, I haven't touched the wine. Nic, have I had any wine this evening?'

'Not that I've seen,' I'd say, diplomatic and cowardly in equal parts.

'Look, I don't need your permission,' she'd snarl at him, 'I'll just help myself.' She'd stand up, a jerky violence in her movements, walk round the table, reach for the flagon, pour herself a glass, go back, sit down, then suddenly shove the full glass away from her, saying: 'Oh, I'm not allowed wine, am I, darling?' She could make 'darling' sound like 'you bastard'.

'Darling,' she'd rant, belligerent, spoiling for a fight.

'Darling, I'm talking to you!' she'd bawl, adding: 'Nic, tell your father I just asked him a question.'

Daddy would keep eating slowly, drink his wine, pour himself more, snigger at her and say: 'I think you've had enough.'

They went on like this all the time. If we had to eat together, I used to memorise items of news I'd heard on the telly, rehearsing them out loud in my room before supper in order to create a conversational diversion. We only had meals if my father came home in time, otherwise Mummy and I helped ourselves to whatever we could find, or she might half cook something and then come out of her room a few hours later to ask whether we'd eaten it or not. There were times when she had no memory for recent events. She'd eat something with me then reappear two hours later to suggest we had a meal.

When they fought at the table, I was more frightened for him than her, especially when she started throwing things. But I understood why his pompous attitude provoked her. One night, after I had gone to bed early, they were arguing. Mild shouting and swearing was followed by the smashing of plates. That I could handle. It didn't hurt, not nearly as much as when they started discussing us, their children, at the tops of their voices.

'How the hell can I leave Nicola here with you, in this

state? And the boys? Why would they want to come home for Christmas?' Daddy.

'There's no way they'd want to go away anywhere with *you*.' Mummy.

'They're children, yet you persist in treating them like adults. Don't think I don't know what goes on when I'm not here, you sending Nicola out to get booze. You're a disgrace. Call yourself a mother. If we ever end up in court, there's no way you'd get custody, no way.' Daddy.

At that point I heard her rummaging in a drawer. I crept closer to the door, peeping just in time to see her pull out a large black kitchen knife and wave it at him, a look of loathing on her face.

'Put it down,' he ordered. 'You're drunk, put it down.'

But she kept waving the knife at him, as if she were looking for somewhere suitable to plunge it. As she raised the knife above her head and appeared to take aim, she swerved and slipped, collapsing to the floor, in a drunken heap. My father grabbed the knife as it bounced and then settled on the floor. He walked out of the kitchen, slowly, clearly shaken, leaving her lying there, crying. She'd always fall asleep after one of their fights, a combination of drink and drugs, prescription drugs mainly. My father once or twice mentioned he would like to leave home. Just the once he left us to live in his caravan on the west coast, but guilt got the better of him and he returned after a few weeks. Generally it never came to anything more than his long weekends away climbing.

I worried about what would happen to her if he left for good. I could stop going to school but that would just attract attention. I had to ask Daddy but I kept finding reasons not to – the main one being he would probably lose his temper. It didn't take much. He'd come in after work, slam the front door so that the noise echoed through the house, and fling his keys down next to an ornamental elephant on the hall table.

'What the hell's for supper?' he'd rasp, never waiting for an answer. He'd strop into his room, slam the door, haul it open two minutes later, march out into the dining room where he'd sit down at the piano to practise. He played the piano like someone without any fingers, banging down on the keys with misshapen stubs. I almost preferred the sound of doors slamming.

I cornered him in his room, one day just before I was sent away to boarding school, by going in on the pretext of dusting it.

'I never thought anyone ever cleaned this room.' He sounded in a good mood for once.

'I don't think they do,' I said. 'It's just that I want to ask you something.'

'Go ahead,' he said, in a way that was supposed to make it easier, but didn't.

I finally blurted out my question: 'What do I do if

something happens to Mummy and you're not here?'

He didn't move. He didn't shout, didn't even look angry; just studiously avoided catching my eye. He sat down in his favourite red velvety armchair. I noticed how haggard he looked, his face like one of the collapsed sponge cakes Dishy was forever pulling out of the oven, disappointment written all over her face. 'Don't think I haven't considered you,' he said. 'I have, long and hard. It's just that sometimes I wonder how much more I can take.' He sighed, examined his nails, a thing he always did when stuck for words. 'And the state of this house . . . I can't stand it, it's filthy. You do your best but you shouldn't be cleaning the house and shopping and God knows what else you do.'

He didn't like going shopping, unless to exotic delicatessens to buy fancy cheeses. He was a typical Frenchman. I never saw him do any housework, other than when he was in Glencoe. I went with him once, maybe twice. There, beneath all that swirling, oppressive mist, he would hum operatic arias, fry sausages in the open air and do all the washing-up and cooking.

'Does she make you do the shopping?' he asked, as if the household had nothing to do with him, which, strictly speaking, it didn't. It ran despite him.

'She doesn't make me,' I said. 'It's just that she can't seem to go out without having a drink first. So, if I do the shopping before school, she doesn't drink. There isn't anyone else. Dishy doesn't do the shopping. It's not part of her work.'

He didn't know I sometimes missed school or turned up late. He always left for work early. There were a lot of things he didn't know and that was the way we liked it.

'She doesn't drink, ha?' he said. 'Not until you've left the house, anyway.'

'I know, Daddy. But I love her.'

He coughed with real embarrassment and turned away from me to tidy some papers on the desk in the corner of his room.

There was so much more I could have said to my father, like how much I loved his room, all his dusty old books, his shoes laid out in a row at the foot of his bed instead of in the wardrobe; the fact that his room didn't have the sickly smell of spilled alcohol like hers. I liked his music collection and would, just once in a while, have enjoyed sitting with him in his room, keeping him company. But he never asked. He sat by himself, night after night after night, year after year. And so did I. Downstairs, in the living room.

'Can't you make her stop drinking?'

'I've tried everything, everything,' he muttered. 'AA have been to the house and talked to her but they say she has to want to stop drinking, otherwise it doesn't work. They said your mother wasn't ready to stop.' He examined his nails again, then added: 'I think she's tried

AA on her own. I know she's been to meetings because she brought some crackpot back here after a meeting a few times, a disgusting woman who lives around here who peed on the settee.'

I wanted to giggle. Nerves. My father didn't do confrontation, which this conversation was to him. Anything personal was no-go territory. He didn't like me to broach the subject of my mother's drinking, for example, but when she was in the Crichton, we often sat together, albeit in silence. One time I made him a book about garden birds. It took about six months to fill it with information in my childish scrawl. Years later, while I watched him clearing out a cupboard on the landing, my bird book fell out onto the floor. He was embarrassed but he actually smiled, a rare smile. It was my one moment in the sun.

And I also wanted to giggle when he talked about the woman who peed on our settee. I knew exactly who he was talking about, indeed dreaded her coming round. He meant Matty.

'I could buy a flat, a small one,' my father was saying. 'I thought you could come and live with me, and the boys, when they come home from school. We could start again.'

He might as well have kicked me in the stomach.

'Move from here? Away from her?'

'Well, you can't have it both ways,' he said, before

realising this sounded too impatient and changing his tone. 'It's just that I worry about what you see and hear. You're so young. I know you can't ask your friends round because you're afraid of what she might do. That's no life.'

'Mummy would die without anyone here.' It was a bald statement but one I thought he needed to hear.

'Your mother needs to come to her senses,' he scoffed. 'The more we stay here, clearing up after her, the more she'll carry on drinking.'

I hated the way he called her 'your mother'.

'Daddy, I couldn't leave her. Of course, I'd want to come and live with you, but I'd worry night and day about her on her own here.'

'I hate coming home to find you sitting in the living room with the TV turned up full blast,' he said.

'Mummy's ill!' I knew I was shouting. 'She's not doing it deliberately. She can't help herself.'

'You don't think so, ha?' was all he said.

It was the first and last real conversation I ever had with my father. After it, I tried to spend more time with my mother. Guilt. But I never really felt at home in her bedroom, too many painful associations: all the terrible fights we'd had in there, the sweet smell of drink and drugs which stung your nostrils, the stains on the bedding. This was where she was slowly drinking herself to death. It was the venue for the worst of her illness and the worst of her recovery. Very little that was good happened in this room and, normally, I spent as little time in there as I could. But, increasingly, it was the only place where I could get to see her. She came out of her room less and less, sometimes went for days without drink and stuffed herself – my father's phrase – with drugs instead. Whenever I went in, I pushed up the rickety window as far as it would go, which annoyed her. She said it compromised the central heating, whatever that meant. I hated the bottles in the wardrobe, squirrelled away inside boots and shoes, which leered out like inquisitors, menacing presence. Empty bottles meant I needed to fish her out the bath, full ones meant I had to challenge her. I wanted to do so with compassion but my inner rage always emerged, no matter how hard I tried to stifle it.

In one corner of her bedroom was a dressing table, covered in loose face powder, Coty, the kind she always wore, and odd bits of expensive jewellery she'd so far avoided selling. A battered chair holding her neatly folded clothes stood in another corner; neatly folded meant she hadn't worn them that day but had floated about in her nightdress. Opposite the bed was a flickering television that was on all the time – her window on the outside world. Her room was crying out for a coat of paint, as was the whole house, with the walls looking more a dirty shade of yellow than the magnolia they had originally been painted.

She was watching Wimbledon the day I steeled myself and went in. She was sober.

'Come in,' she said, patting the bed. 'Come and watch this match. It's brilliant.'

My mother was sitting on the bed, not in her usual prone position. It was rare to see her sitting up, engaging with people or with the telly. She was wearing old trousers and a pink shirt. I gave her a kiss on the cheek and retreated, happy because I couldn't detect any smell of booze.

'I've been watching them eat strawberries and cream,' she went on. 'It's making me hungry.'

'Shall I go out and get some?' My enthusiasm rarely enjoyed an outing these days. When it did, it burst into the sunshine after a long period in hibernation.

'Will you?' She reached for her bag and pulled out her wallet. 'Here's a ten-pound note, Nic. Get strawberries, cream and some chocolate. Let's go mad. Make sure you inspect the strawbs first for bruises.'

I ran to my room, changed out of school uniform into my jeans and a jumper. Looking into the mirror, I was surprised to see a girl with a smiling face.

'Hurry and I'll make some tea,' she called from her bedroom, a voice so bright, so cheerful, so unlike my mother, it made me want to weep.

When I came back, laden with goodies, she had already made tea, put two mugs on a tray and was sitting on her bed again, waiting. I went to the kitchen, washed the strawberries with care and arranged them into two bowls, adding a generous amount of cream. I put a bar of chocolate on the tray and carried it through to her room. I sat on the side of the bed and watched her, rather than the telly.

'Nic, I've been thinking. It's your birthday next week. You're eleven.' Mummy popped a strawberry into her mouth. 'Yummy. These are so sweet. I'm a sucker for sweet things, especially when I'm not . . .'

'Mummy,' I cut in, not in the mood to discuss drink, 'what were you going to say about my birthday?'

'Well, I wanted to know whether you fancied some new clothes. I had wondered whether we could go into town together and have a look, but I'm not sure I'm up to doing that.'

I swallowed a strawberry, saying nothing, staring blankly at the beige carpet, worried about the look of hurt I'd seen in her eyes. She thought I was too ashamed to go with her and she was right. I didn't mind being seen with her in the street but in shops, for some reason, I did get embarrassed. There was no point in denying it. If only she'd stay sober. But what were the chances of that? She had become so nervy and anxious lately, that there was talk among her doctors of giving her a lobotomy, or a 'fullbottleinfrontofme', as we children called it. She was delighted at the prospect, as was my father, yet they both knew such an operation would leave her as dull as a vegetable. She thought this would be the release she needed, that she wouldn't need to drink and she'd be happy at last. My father just didn't care any more. He'd prefer a vegetable for a wife than a drunk. But Peter and I were horrified at the prospect. She had once introduced me to a woman she knew who'd had the same operation. The woman just sat staring straight ahead – smiling blankly, with no thoughts, no contribution to make.

Mummy was still on about my birthday.

'I'll just give you the money, then,' she mumbled. She hadn't meant it unkindly but her words made me feel guilty.

'Mummy, if you'd like to come, we could get some clothes for you, too,' I tried.

'Oh, I don't need clothes these days. I never go out.'

'You could. You look fabulous when you dress up.'

'You think? But this is about you. What will you buy, darling?'

'I want some new jeans, maybe some make-up.' I watched her eyes widen. 'I might even buy a watch. I've been meaning to ask for that for a while.'

She laughed. 'When I was your age, young lady, I didn't even get pocket money.'

She was in the mood for talking. When she was sober, she seemed to realise how lonely she really was, and how lonely I was, both of us cooped up in our own little prisons. I loved to listen to her talk about her life, but only when she was sober.

'When did you have your first boyfriend, Mummy?' That question always got her going.

'It wasn't him, you know,' she jerked her head in the direction of my father's room. 'I met my first boyfriend at school. He followed me around for years, like a puppy, before he asked me out. I can still remember our first date because we went skating. I fell over. There I was sprawled all over the ice rink, knickers showing, no dignity left. I thought he'd never ask me out again, but he did.' She pulled herself further up the bed, leaning back against the pillows. 'He went away to college eventually. Maybe I should have stuck with him.'

'Daddy's not so bad,' I said, cleaning the cream off my bowl with the spoon.

'Claude is a good man,' she said slowly. 'Basically, he is a loyal man. It's just that he doesn't cope well with mental illness . . .'

I interrupted: 'Mummy, look at that guy serve. It's amazing.'

She sighed and looked at the television, sipped her tea and smiled. It was nice, just the two of us relaxing in her room.

'I'll never get a boyfriend,' I said.

'Of course you will. Your father always says they'll be falling over themselves to get to you.' I was taken aback when she said that. It was unbelievable! Considering the number of times he criticised me about the way I looked, it also seemed highly unlikely.

'I'm so odd, though,' was all I could think of to say. 'I don't want to go out and drink cider in the park and smoke like my friends.'

'I should think not,' Mummy said sharply. 'Not at your age.'

'That's what my age group do nowadays.'

'You mean the boys go off with the girls who drink?' she asked.

I shook my head. Hearing drops of rain against the window, I stood up to close it. There was a distant rumble and the sun was fading in an overcast sky. The couple next door were outside in the garden, seated in green plastic chairs, each with a drink in their hand, looking so respectable. They had noticed the patter of rain and were preparing to saunter inside. We would never sit outside and have a drink like that – too busy scooping it out of the cistern where nobody could see. I sat down on the bed again and found myself wondering whether she would make it sober into next week. It would be a record if she did.

'Can I get a pair of jeans, Mummy?'

'Of course you can and gym shoes as well. I've got jeans in the wardrobe,' she added, smiling.

'You're joking.'

'No, really.' She almost looked excited.

I watched her jump off the bed, open the wardrobe door, rummage around and then pull a pair of faded denims off a wooden hanger. She sat on the bed, stepped into them and hauled them up, struggling for several minutes with the zip.

'God, I've put on weight since I last wore these.' She turned for me to inspect.

'You look fantastic,' I said and meant it. 'You look ten years younger. We should go out on the town.'

She laughed. 'I think I'll keep them on.' She opened a drawer, found a black jumper with a plunging neckline which she put on and walked over to her dressing table, brushed her long hair, pinned it back and put on her favourite earrings. I found myself wishing my father was in, just so he could catch a glimpse of her like this. She was unrecognisable.

'Okay, let's go and have a drink,' she said. Seeing my face fall, she continued quickly, 'I've got ginger beer or Coke. Which would you prefer?'

'I'll get it. I'll bring it through to the sitting room.'

I went to the kitchen, filled her a glass with ginger beer, put in some ice, grabbed a Coke for myself and carried them both through to the sitting room. We sat together, chatting.

'I find it hard to make friends with boys,' I said. 'Girls are much easier because you can be yourself. With boys,

I'm always worried about how I look – and they laugh at the way I walk, anyway. I think I'll always need treatment on my legs.'

'They wouldn't laugh at your legs if they knew what you'd been through,' she said. 'I told you I was fifteen when I first went out with a boy,' she said, 'and nervous. I stayed with him until I left school because I was too scared to go out with anyone else. My father always told me I was attractive, so I don't know why I lacked confidence. You would have loved my father . . .'

My mother loved to talk about her father, Sir Maurice Craig. I don't know how many times she told me he was psychiatrist to the royal family, especially to Edward VIII just before he abdicated. She had this amazing photograph of him. I still have it. Sir Maurice Craig is walking along beside King George VI, past a large crowd. I never met my maternal grandfather, who died in 1935, but he was a handsome man: sober, tall, distinguished, with snowy white hair and deep-set brown eyes. His wife, Edith, had been a debutante. She came out, was presented to the Queen and had been a real good-time girl. A lousy mother, though.

'My father treated Leonard and Virginia Woolf,' she'd say. Then we'd chime together, 'He treated a lot of prominent people,' and she'd laugh, knowing she'd given me the same information a thousand times. I discovered only a few years ago that the doctors in *Mrs Dalloway* were based on Sir Maurice Craig. He was one of seven children. His father had been a GP in Edinburgh and a morphine addict. By way of explanation for her drinking, my mother always said: 'You see, Nic, it skips a generation.'

'Your father wasn't much help to you two, though, was he?' I said that day, pouring my ever-large glass of cold water over our conversation. By 'you two' I meant his daughters, who both became alcoholics. My mother's sister, Alison, also had the problem, although not to the same degree. She was younger, always seemed more able to cope. They had a brother, Peter, who my mother adored. As children, their parents were rarely with them but farmed them out to nannies, governesses and servants. At bedtime, a nanny would escort Monica, Peter and Alison to the drawing room to say goodnight, and, on many days, that was the only contact between the children and their parents.

Aunt Alison died in a horrendous car crash in the eighties, along with her husband Alex, a GP in Swanage, leaving three daughters. They didn't visit us very often as children, mainly because my father felt our house was fit for no one, not even relatives. My mother had worshipped her father, even though she saw him so seldom. 'The problem was,' she said, 'he was never at home. His consulting practice, in Harley Street, was the largest of his time.'

What she didn't often say was that he had prescribed Valium for both his daughters when they were just fifteen. This made her angry in later life, yet she blamed her mother, Edith, for her chronic lack of confidence. She used to tell a story about a dream she'd had, in which she was sitting, crying, in the drawing room of the family home in Somerset. When her mother and sister asked her what was wrong, she replied: 'My psychiatrist says I shall have to spend the rest of my life in a mental hospital.' Edith just stared at her; and when my mother asked if she wanted her to leave home the reply was: 'Yes, immediately.' She sensed that her mother didn't have time for her and preferred her younger daughter. My mother also swore that taking Valium, those 'little blue demons', marked the start of her downfall. For the rest of her life, she needed something to calm her down, as if a state of relaxation was hers by right. When Valium wasn't available, drink brought the same effect with the added attraction that you didn't have to ask anyone to write out a prescription.

If she got bored with the subject of her father, her other favourite topic was how alike we were. 'I'm afraid you're so like me, Nicola', she'd say. When I'd frown, she'd add, 'That doesn't mean you'll be a drunk, darling, of course not.' She laughed when she said it but the words hurt all the same. That was a conversation stopper as far as I was concerned. I worried endlessly about ending up a drunk, finishing up like her. Out of all of us, at that time, I was the one most like my mother in terms of vulnerability.

It had been a good girls-together chat with my mother, curled up on her bed drinking ginger beer and Coke, but then I decided to go and do some homework in my room. My father hadn't come back from his climbing, so I'd get some peace. When he was at home, it was impossible to relax. I'd be too busy waiting for the next explosion. A couple of hours later, I felt so tired I undressed, had a bath and popped through to say goodnight to my mother. She wasn't in the sitting room, so I gently pushed open the door to her bedroom and peered round to call goodnight.

The sickly smell hit me straight away. She was half on the bed, half off, snoring heavily, semi-dressed, jeans round her ankles, bum naked and bruised. She'd been trying to get herself into bed. I threw open the door, went over to her bedside table, picked up the glass of ginger beer I'd given her and sniffed it – gin. On the floor lay her bottle of sickly syrup, Largactil. She'd had both. We'd tried to stop her doctor prescribing Largactil, a drug commonly used on people in institutions who didn't have the power to say no. It was used on Mummy because she couldn't relax – not even in her own home. It was stronger than Valium or Librium, both of which she took from time to time. She chopped and changed drugs as if they were socks or shoes.

I put down the glass and left the room, slamming the door so loudly it rattled on its hinges. There wasn't a sound from her after that.

I went to watch TV and flicked from channel to channel, my stomach gurgling in rebellion. Then, I got up, stretched out and ambled to the kitchen where Mummy had earlier left three plates on the table, plus a knife and fork and a cup and saucer at each place. What an optimist she was. The table would still be set the following morning, untouched. On the mahogany sideboard under the window sat a cracked wooden chopping board on which lay a tired lettuce, three tomatoes, a cucumber and three eggs, recently hard-boiled. I knew how they would be arranged on the plates – exactly as they were on the chopping board. If we were really lucky, Mummy might remember to remove the clingfilm. In my heart of hearts, I suppose I knew she was trying but, as a child, you don't give credit where it's due. It takes the wisdom that comes with age to do that.

I saw something move behind the lettuce, a brown tail, a bony, flicking thing, worm-like and leathery. One tiny claw was visible. I hated that scrabbling noise. Mice terrified me because they were so small, because they darted around the kitchen, scurrying into cupboards before disappearing altogether. Although I didn't see them that often, the bloody creatures had taken up permanent residence in our kitchen almost to the extent of leaving shopping lists around so we'd know what they wanted to eat. They were every bit as comfortable in the house as we were. Mummy always said she'd do something about them, call in Rentokil or something, but she never got round to it. Daddy used to tell me the mice were sweet, to imagine them as little Beatrix Potter characters dressed in summer bonnets and gingham dresses, but I couldn't. His attitude angered me. He was a doctor. Why couldn't he see my point of view? Why didn't he care? When I saw mice, I saw dirt. I saw the squalor of our lives.

Mummy would saunter across the greasy kitchen floor in her grubby nightdress, spilling bits of cheese all over the place, never thinking to clean up after herself. The sink usually contained the previous week's washing-up water: stained cups floated near the top, unwashed pans sat on the bottom. Up until the age of ten, I would put on her apron, which drowned me, and stand at the sink for hours, scrubbing dishes, surfaces, anything that caught my eye.

Now I was that bit older, I kept my oldest jeans and jumper for cleaning the kitchen. I'd still scrub until I sweated, until my nails flaked and the skin on my hands smarted. I was obsessive about hygiene. Although my mother didn't eat proper meals, she picked at food all the time, left scraps lying around. If Dishy left a fish pie, which she often did, my mother would emerge from her room, hungry, scoop out huge spoonfuls and then forget to put the dish back in the fridge, leaving it lying there on the worktop, half eaten, unpalatable. Poor Dishy. She tried so hard to make us normal but failed at every booze-ridden turn.

The mouse sounded much louder now, though I could no longer see it. I knew what I had to do. It was going to be one of those evenings. I tackled the washing-up piled high in the sink. Once that was finished, I left it to drip-dry and, with my chapped hands lost in an enormous pair of rubber gloves, wrenched open a cupboard door, pulled out a red bucket, mop and scrubbing brush. My hands were in a terrible state from cleaning. Sometimes I wore gloves but they only aggravated the dermatitis.

Daddy always said I was the one person who could make the kitchen glisten, so I cleaned until my fingers ached. I moved on to the floor. Bleach was the only way to get rid of vermin. I filled the bucket with scorching water, added some liquid soap and bleach and scrubbed, every few minutes soaking the mop, ramming its head against the plastic sieve to remove any excess moisture, imagining the imprint of my mother's face beneath. I scrubbed and scrubbed until sweat trickled down my cheeks and puddles collected round my lower back. By the time I'd finished, the floor, sink and taps gleamed. I pushed and pulled the mop, throwing my fraught body into the motion. I felt my back and thighs ache, but that only spurred me on to do more. Clean, clean, clean away the booze, said the voice inside my head, the leftovers, half-cooked meals abandoned after heavy drinking sessions and never served to anybody; the waste, the family life that never was. It all went down the same plug hole.

When I stopped for a cup of tea, the kitchen was the way my soul demanded it be. Seeing clean surfaces allowed me to breathe again. Food was either put away in the fridge or locked in cupboards. There were no unwashed plates lying around, no scraps on the floor to slip on whenever I walked in, hungry and unsuspecting. By now I was ravenous. The thought of tiptoeing upstairs and into my mother's room when she was drunk in bed and helping myself to her money always made me nervous, but I reckoned I deserved it after all that scrubbing.

As I climbed the stairs, I wondered what she'd been drinking today, which particular smell would hit me when I opened her bedroom door. Vodka? It was usually vodka or gin. Sometimes the reek included some kind of syrupy drug that she drank like a cocktail. Melleril, it was called. It had a horrible cloying smell that made me want to vomit. There was a rumour going round at school that she wrote her own prescriptions. I knew it was doing the rounds because someone told me without realising I was her daughter.

'So, you're Nicola?' she'd said after dropping her precious bombshell, as if I were some sort of dog turd someone had warned her not to stand in. 'How do you cope with having a mother like that?' After a long pause, she added: 'Someone should report her to the police.'

I could get so angry on my mother's behalf, away from her. Yet, two minutes in her company and my rage was directed straight at her.

I tiptoed to her room, turned the door handle slowly, grabbed it so it didn't flick back, held the handle as still as possible then pushed open the door; crept in across the faded blue carpet, feet sinking into lush pile, clocking the stench of stale alcohol, cigarette smoke and the tranquilliser syrup stuff. Her discarded jeans were lying on the floor, her former laughing self completely gone.

My mother's room looked out over the neighbours' parked cars and a red pillar box. I kept offering to paint her room a cheerful colour but she never agreed. The décor suited her outlook on life: jaundiced, sallow. Her double bed sagged in the middle from years of sleeping alone and too often. The bedside table with its chipped marble surface, a decorative blend of bluebirds and plants, was always covered in globules of Steradent, face powder and spilt medicine. There were three chests of drawers in the room, all covered in dust. They contained old clothes and bottles of spirits, empty and full. In one corner of the room was a flickering black-and-white television, which was left switched on until it made a piercing noise at closing-down time when I'd have to race through and switch it off – though she always managed to sleep right through it.

While peering at the gently snoring figure of my mother, I had to stifle a cough. Her handbag was lying right next to the bed, just under her sleeping form. I crept closer, within inches of the bag. Just behind it was an overturned gin bottle, its dregs seeping out onto the carpet, forming a dark, wet pool. I was surprised she allowed herself to miss even the smallest drop. I knelt down, my face right up close to hers. Her eyes were closed, the wrinkles clearly visible by the light of the small bedside lamp, as well as remnants of orange make-up that had run from her cheeks into her damp matted hair. She was forty-five going on eighty. She just lay there.

Despite her blowsy appearance, sagging cheeks, lines etched deeply into her forehead, of pain and sacrifice, of rejection and self-loathing, she looked almost serene. I wanted to reach out and put my arms around her, tell her for the first time in years that I loved her, forgave her. But that familiar sickly-sweet smell from her lips ensured mine stayed shut tight. I hated that smell. It stood for everything bad between her and me. I would make that step, try so hard to forgive, only to be forced to recoil, to take that sudden step backwards in the knowledge that, yet again, she'd let me down. She drank all day, cheap sherry, wine at mealtimes and anything my father left lying around, such as a half carafe of his home-made wine. She would drink it then water it down, thinking he wouldn't notice.

We always had the same conversation. 'Mummy, you've got to stop drinking like this,' I'd say. 'You'll kill yourself.'

'Darling, Nic, I haven't been drinking today. I swear.'

'I can smell it.'

'Whatever you smell, it's not alcohol, darling.'

Of course, she was right. It wasn't alcohol. It was some drug or other. Our arguments always went this way, round and round in circles, circumnavigating the truth, making detours, until I'd be forced to give up, exhausted, angry, disappointed. And she could turn away from me, a little smile of triumph across her battered cheeks.

I sat back on my heels and delved into the handbag, pulling out a torn cream wallet which I unzipped in near-total silence. There was a lot of silver inside the purse. It took all my nerve to explore further, to prise open the little leather folds and see whether she had any pound notes, even a few tenners, perhaps. One time I found a twenty. Stealing that twenty-pound note was the biggest thrill ever. It wasn't stealing, I told myself when I couldn't sleep at night. To hell! I was her daughter, her child. It was her duty as a mother to feed, clothe and love me. I needed to carry out these tasks for myself and I couldn't live on fresh air. Daddy would make one of his cassoulets if I waited and asked him nicely, but I didn't feel like big wads of garlic. I didn't know any kids who ate fancy cassoulets full of garlic for their tea. Why should I?

Actually I had quite a lot of money stashed away. I'd put the money in a drawer in my bedroom, in the small chest beside my bed, like a nest egg, my only real possession, my own little stash. The truth was I loved stealing from her, but have never been tempted to steal from anybody else. With my mother, it was like taking something back, or trying to – something I couldn't get any other way.

I'll never forget the time she caught me in the act. She must have been pretending to be drunk and that was so unusual. I might have known by the fact that there was no syrupy smell in the bedroom. The air wasn't fresh. It just wasn't as stale and cloying as usual. That should have stopped me in my tracks, but the desire to get one up on her was overwhelming. I had to take something out of her bag. As I released the catch with a soft click, she raised one eyelid, never said a word then lowered it in a flash. Sharp for a drunk. My slender hand was embedded in one of the folds of her wallet. I knew she was watching as I removed a ten-pound note, silently closed the wallet and then sneaked from the room. There was no point in changing my plan and sneaking out empty-handed. It had already gone too far. Maybe I'd wanted her to see me; my way of letting her know I felt that she owed me something.

My mother never tackled me about it, never even said in the way people do when they've been burgled: 'I swear I had a ten-pound note in my wallet.' She may have wanted me to sweat out my guilt. If so, her wish came true. I thought about little else apart from the voice inside my head that kept telling me I stole from my own mother.

# Chapter 8

# Forgive Me, Mother

My first communion succeeded in weaning my mother off the bottle for a few weeks. She was determined to be in a fit state to leave the house and be there in the church to see me receive the bread and wine, a sacrament of initiation to her faith, as she saw it. We went to Mass most Sundays, in relays. My father raced out of the house first, to catch the early service. Otherwise, he maintained, going to church ruined his whole day. 'Get it over and done with,' was his weekly greeting to the God of his choice.

There were rehearsals galore, in our church, just off Ravelston Dykes in Murrayfield. We, the first communicants, had to be shown off to the parish. This involved sitting in pews in the front row and standing up for a blessing every so often, kneeling down, standing up again. My mother called it 'ecclesiastical PE'.

The truth was she cared desperately about me making my first communion. She wanted me to make a go of it because no one ever looked up to her or sought to follow in her footsteps – mainly because they didn't usually lead anywhere. In the case of the Church, she had opened a door she considered important and desperately wanted me, at the very least, to go through it behind her.

She was, or rather, had been, a devout Catholic; a convert to be precise. Before she'd married, she'd been nothing, an agnostic of sorts. When she married my father and became more and more miserable, she eventually turned to a priest for help. She says he saved her life; he didn't stop her drinking, but he did make her believe again. I think they had an affair. My father certainly thought so. He loathed this priest, once accusing him of helping himself to wine from the cupboard and not for communion, either. I was never sure how close my mother was to him, but he was often in the house when my father was at work. She wanted me to be brought up a Catholic; indeed, she insisted on it, despite my father not being that keen.

I hadn't a clue what I was going to say to the priest in my first confession, which I had to make before receiving communion. My repertoire of sins was limited to 'I thought nasty things about someone' or 'I used bad language.'

Stealing from my mother would qualify, of course,

but I fully intended keeping quiet about that one, imagining it would cast me in a very dark light. More to the point, my justifications for periodically removing a few pounds from her purse were fine with me. I was quite happy to accept the legitimacy of my reasons, but not sure a priest would. His view was unlikely to be as lenient as my own. A priest would be sure to condemn me to endless rosaries or, worse, eternal damnation. Just as well no priest knew about the ten-pound notes. God knows what sort of punishment that would have invited. I justified it by telling myself I had to eat. But it wasn't that. It was the actual act of taking from my mother. It gave me a feeling which I now know was revenge.

Occasionally, as my big day approached, my mother would offer to help me rehearse for my first confession. There was a large, roomy cupboard off her bedroom where she kept the clothes and shoes she never wore, preferring to stick to her functional black trousers and green cardigan. She called this her 'slopping about' attire. Slopped over, more like. The cardy, in particular, was covered in tea, coffee, wine and various foods. She would sometimes stand in the kitchen, spilling baked beans down her front as she spooned them out of a tin.

One day, about a week before my official debut in the confessional box, we decided to use the roomy cupboard to practise in. We took in two chairs, one for the priest, the other for the sinner, and placed them one on either side of the clothes rail. I draped a long, dark counterpane over the rail. It hung between us, rendering the experience far more realistic than I would have liked; the only concession to reality being Mummy's mouldy slippers visible beneath the hemline. She was to be the father confessor and I the hopeless sinner. She thought this hilarious, delighted to see our roles reversed – not to be the black sheep for once, even if it was only for ten minutes. At first, the partition, the awesome silences in the cupboard and her deep voice were so realistic I found I was too nervous to speak. She kept calling me 'my child', humming and hawing and mumbling away to herself like a distracted old man.

'How long is it since your last confession, my child?' she asked.

'This is my first confession, Father.'

'Have you been having any evil thoughts?' This came out in a creepy voice I had never heard her use before.

'No, Father.'

'Are you sure now, child? You haven't been wishing your mother would fall off a high cliff into the sea or anything like that?'

'No, Father.' I was giggling now.

'Have you been thinking about boys at all, child?'

'Sometimes, Father; nothing bad, though.'

'Have you had naughty thoughts? D'you know what I mean, child?' I heard her stifle a giggle.

The question embarrassed me so much I tried to change the subject straight away, without thinking, and succeeded.

'I've stolen money, Father.' The words were out before I could stop them. If only I'd had the courage to stay with the naughty thoughts, this would have been safer ground, even with Mummy. One of the nuns at school said she could always tell a girl who had naughty thoughts about boys because she didn't look people straight in the face. I certainly never looked her straight in the face again.

'God help us. Who could you possibly have stolen money from?' came the aggressive response.

'Someone in my family,' I muttered.

'How many people are there in your family?'

'There's me and my brothers and my mother, er, and father.'

It was out before I could stop it. Tears, scarcely having time to gather, began to run down my burning cheeks. It wasn't so much that I was sorry. It was the fact that I was making her feel even more rejected than she already did; some achievement! She already lived beneath a large stone, lowest of the low life. Now I was standing on that stone, jumping up and down on it.

'Do you know why you steal from your mother?' She asked sharply. She'd dropped the mock-priest tone and sounded angry and hurt.

I could feel the truth lurking somewhere out there and was sure she did too. I could hear this fact in her voice. Its pitch was raised, full of expectancy. She was willing me to tell her why I'd sinned against her.

'I, er, it's . . . Sometimes I feel I have to take something from her because she won't give me what I . . .'

'Is it because your mother's a no-good drunk, my child? Is that what you think?'

The voice, now convincingly masculine, sounded a touch defensive.

'You know as well as I do, Father,' I said, hoping to skirt the issue, 'that nothing excuses stealing. No matter what you think of someone, what is theirs is theirs and no one has any right to remove it. I could give you any one of the reasons I use to justify my stealing but none of them would satisfy you. They're excuses anyway, not reasons. I take from my mother because it makes me feel better when nothing else does. Absolutely nothing. Will that do?'

There was an awful silence. I could tell she was devastated. I might as well have stabbed her through the heart. I swear she was crying behind the partition. I hadn't said it to hurt her, but that's what she would think. She had foolishly been fishing for information and didn't like what she saw jumping about on the end of her rod.

I wished she'd pursue the naughty thoughts line of questioning, though I couldn't bear the idea of discussing sex with her, even if she was disguised as a priest. Mummy only ever talked about it when she was drunk and then she only talked about her one or two experiences with Daddy, which wasn't exactly sex education. She had never told me about periods. A girl in my class told me after I was horrified at discovering blood between my legs and thought my insides were falling out. It was the worst thing my mother had done, or not done. She was a doctor, yet she hadn't bothered telling me the facts of life.

The cupboard stank of old coats and unwashed clothing. I tried to see them, take in their pattern and design – anything rather than continue this unwanted conversation, but darkness meant that only talk or embarrassing silence could prevail.

'Anyway,' I said firmly, 'even if Mummy is drunk occasionally, and I do take her money sometimes, I love her more than anybody else in the world.'

I could hear my priest breathe in, almost gasp.

'Say that again,' she said. 'Please.'

I started to speak, but nothing came. We must have sat like that for half an hour, not moving, buried in our respective morasses of thought, as if frozen in time and space; not unpleasant, but ice can be so difficult to break.

'I absolve you from your sins,' she said, eventually. 'In the name of the Father, the Son and the Holy Ghost.'

With that, my mother swept out of the cupboard, in

the way religious people do, leaving me to hug my knees in the dark until I heard her go into the kitchen to make a cup of tea – my cue to stumble out into the well-lit bedroom. She had had her moment of truth.

# Chapter 9

# Falling Down Drunk

One October evening, shortly before my $11^+$ exam, I'd been in front of the telly for three hours, still wearing my school blazer. The rain was hammering down outside and the house was as quiet as a crypt. Mummy was upstairs, drunk, asleep, or both. She had thrown open all the windows after one of her frenzied spates of cleaning, which took place in the middle of the night and were extremely noisy. I don't know what had brought this one on. Generally, if she cleaned, she had run out of drink and it was some kind of displacement activity. It was also a rare event. In our house, everything boasted a thick layer of filth, even us. But I kept the sitting room spotless because it was my patch, my oasis of calm. I cleaned and dusted it every morning, polishing the table beside my chair. It was important because it was where I sat.

'See what a good mother I am?' was what her back said when she cleaned. 'See how well I look after you?' Then she'd retire into her room, crying, saying nobody would help her, that she couldn't cope with the house because it was too big. It made me so angry, the way she was always trying to prove she was a good mother. She was no mother at all.

'See what a fucking drunk I am? See what a useless cow? See how I trip over you when I'm not looking where I'm going?' I muttered. She was getting on my nerves, asking, no, begging more like it, for trouble.

Thankfully, her cleaning frenzy had stopped. No more humming Hoovers, no more dusters hovering over soiled tables and chairs, no more attempts to gain my approval. That afternoon, she'd been in the kitchen baking a cake. The last time she baked a cake, about a year before, during the school holidays, the smell of burnt raisins hung in the air for weeks, prompting a joke from my father, not normally one for funny stories. That time, she had left the cake in the oven and gone upstairs to drink, leaving me in to complete her masterpiece. I phoned my father, who was at the hospital, to ask how you knew when a cake was ready. He was angry at first, because I'd disturbed his work over something so minor. He soon relented, though, and said: 'Well, you open the oven door, then take a knife and stick it in the cake. If it comes out clean, the cake's ready. By the way, if it comes out clean, take the rest of the cutlery and stick it in there as well.'

I thought it was hilarious and laughed loud and long. I'd never shared a joke with him before. It was the truth of it that made me laugh so much. All the knives and forks were coated in grease and the plates stained; dirt had collected under the oven, behind the fridge, in the food cupboards; the sink was always full of stale, brown water, and, of course, there were the mice. They scampered about during the night: pompous, plump, distinctly Edinburgh mice, well fed and certainly well educated in the art of scavenging.

This time, I had saved the cake again. It sat on the kitchen worktop, unfinished, uneaten. We hadn't yet eaten anything and I was considering helping myself to some of the dry sponge when I heard the suction sound of a cork unscrewing upstairs, a noise I loathed. She tended to drink wine last thing. Sometimes she'd stumble about and fall, then shout for me to pick her up, but not tonight, just this loud silence. Then I heard a crash from the kitchen, a cup or glass, yet more broken pieces to pave the way to the kettle.

'Hey, darling,' her voice pierced my thoughts a moment later, its tone uncertain.

'You've had your supper . . . I cooked it, didn't I?' Mummy, who had appeared in the doorway, came to lean over me, breath stinking of wine and sherry, stroking my hair, her brow furrowed, eyes glazed, speaking in that tone which told me she didn't know whether it was day or night. I kissed her quickly on the cheek, tried not to recoil like my father did when I kissed him. It was the same every single night. The script never changed. But the time it did, it was one hell of a shock.

The next day I arrived home from school and found I couldn't get into the house. At first I was furious because, through the hazy glass, I could see the door was blocked by something large and brown, like a box. I assumed it was bottles of wine or cooking sherry. She had ordered boxes of wine before, then been unable to carry them upstairs. I turned my key, pushing hard, but the door refused to budge. I toyed with the idea of charging at it – like I'd seen my father do – but knew I'd end up hurting myself. I wondered why my mother didn't answer the door; she wasn't usually drunk to the point of collapse at this time in the afternoon. I was used to finding her in her bedroom and trying to chat to her about my day, then, on not getting a response, going and making myself a cup of tea.

The truth hit me as fiercely as a fist between the eyes. The brown blur on the other side of the glass-panelled door was her, motionless, possibly dead. That was all I could think. Perhaps she had tripped and fallen. She was always falling over and this time she'd gone too far. I didn't know what to do. I didn't want the neighbours involved in case I was taken into care – which was not part of my grand plan. I wanted Jo's parents to adopt me or for somebody to come into the house every day, just to see if I was all right. I didn't want to be put in some institution with other kids who didn't have disabilities and who wouldn't understand me. Ideally, I wanted Mr Scott to admit me, on a permanent basis, to hospital. That would have been my dream come true: seeing him every day, having nice meals with kids I liked, having cups of tea and painkillers brought to me in the middle of the night, when I couldn't sleep, by nurses who said they loved me.

I walked to the nearest phone box and dialled 999. I gave my name and address and said my mother was lying at the foot of the stairs, blocking the front door. No sooner had I returned to the house than an ambulance arrived, siren blaring, with the police close behind – so much for not wanting to alert the neighbours to a crisis in the Barry household. An officer smashed the front window, clambering through the shattered pane into the dining room. I held my breath. Within minutes he was bending over my mother. He opened the door to let the ambulance crew in.

'Your mother's asking for you,' the policeman said, grinning.

I burst into tears and started breathing again, anger already beginning to stir. Once in the hallway, I could see she was drunk rather than hurt by any fall. She was lying on her back in a torn nightdress, one leg in front, the other tucked beneath her. Her arms were folded over her chest, her face tear-stained and bruised from the fall.

'I'm sorry,' she began the minute she saw me. 'Nic, I'm so sorry. I slipped on the stair carpet. I didn't mean to . . .'

The men gently moved her onto a stretcher. As she lay there, tears still flowing, I put my arms around her and hugged her for the first time in years, amazed at the sense of relief I felt. 'I thought you were dead,' I said. 'Poor Mummy, poor, poor Mummy.'

'Wishful thinking,' she replied, smiling. 'Could I have a glass of water?'

'Not for you, dear,' the ambulance driver said firmly. 'You may need an operation.'

'Did you go upstairs for a sleep or something?' I asked and she looked at me, without answering. I bet she'd been looking for Daddy's secret stash of drink. Not such a bloody secret, more an open invitation. He hated her drunk but, even more, he hated her sober. It was a mystery to me why he didn't hide the wine he made. It was sick. He was sick. I suppose we all were.

'I want to come with you,' I said to the ambulance crew. They exchanged a glance.

'Maybe wait for your dad,' one of the crew said.

'No. He's a doctor. I don't know when he'll be back.' The bastard, as Mummy called him, should have been here. He would have known what to do. It was his job.

Don't know why I told them he was a doctor. I suppose to shame him or something like that.

'Okay, hop in the back with her, then.'

The man lifted me up into the back of the ambulance where I sat on a bunk bed opposite my mother's stretcher. As I settled into the small space, a reek of gin filled my nostrils and the affection I'd been feeling for her faded fast. A few minutes before, I'd been so glad she wasn't dead. Now, here I was, once again wishing she were. She'd made out she was a poor soul, that she'd tripped on the carpet. Yeah, she'd bloody tripped all right, because she couldn't see where she was going, because she was half-cut as usual. I wanted to ask them to stop the ambulance, chuck her out on the grass verge, stop wasting their time, my time. I could feel my shoulders shrinking back into their normal position. For a few moments outside, they had loosened, allowing my arms the freedom to embrace her. Now they were closing in on my chest again, like the pincers of a crab. My whole back was rigid with tension. That was how I walked around. What was she playing at?

'Name's Jim,' said the ambulance man who'd helped me, holding out his hand. I took it and was surprised at how warm and strong his grasp felt. I held onto his hand while we looked into each other's eyes. His were a soft brown, the surrounding skin crinkly at the edges, as if he laughed a lot. I noticed a dark stubble on his chin when he wiped a few drops of sweat from his brow.

'How much does she drink?' Jim didn't look away like most people did when they asked questions like that.

I glanced at Mummy. She was snoring loudly.

'She can't hear us,' he added. 'She must have had a bucket today, anyway.'

'She drinks a lot,' I mumbled. 'She's a doctor.' I'd done it again, shared information for no reason.

'They're the worst,' Jim confided. 'Trust me, I've seen more piss artists among the medics than . . . is it gin she drinks?'

'Gin, vodka, wine, sherry. You name it.'

'They think vodka doesn't smell,' Jim said, adding with a grin, 'and it absolutely stinks. It always reminds me of the smell of two-star petrol, not that I've ever drunk any.'

I smiled.

'So it's just you and your mum at home?' Jim asked, but not in the 'you-should-be-in-care' voice I dreaded.

'No. My brothers are there some of the time, when they're not away at school, and my father.'

'Full-time job looking after her, I bet?'

I smiled at him, aware that I wanted to burst into tears again. He was kind. He reached above my mother's body for a thermos flask.

'Only tea, I'm afraid.' Jim filled a plastic cup and handed me a hot, stewed brew.

'It's probably too strong, but it'll make you feel better. Have you had anything to eat since you got home?'

'Nope.'

'Used to that, I expect?' Jim turned to look at my mother with more sympathy than I thought she deserved. 'We'll get you a plate of fish and chips or something at the hospital. They'll need to keep her in overnight, just in case,' he added. 'They'll let you stay with her, if you want, in a spare bed they use for families. You can phone your dad from the hospital.'

'I don't know.' I looked at the floor of the ambulance. 'He'd be furious if he knew, embarrassed as well – in case anyone he knows at the hospital has to look after her. It's pathetic.' I spat out the last word. 'He worries about his reputation.'

'Quite right,' Jim said. 'People look up to doctors, you know, don't want them falling off their pedestals.'

He stopped talking as we turned into the hospital's main drive then put his arm around my shoulders. I did cry then. I wasn't used to adults behaving like adults. I wasn't used to the kindness or the attention. When I didn't get it, I was fine. I didn't cry a lot as a child. But when I grew up, it was as if I never stopped.

The ambulance drew up at the entrance to casualty. I stayed close to Jim, inhaling his pleasant odour of sweat and tobacco, and found myself wishing he were mine. My father, I mean. When the crew lowered the stretcher and carried it inside, we stayed in the back of the ambulance for a few minutes.

'Have you got a nice GP?' he asked.

'Yep.' I was sobbing now.

'Check it out. Ask your parents to make an appointment for you. Go see your GP and tell him or her how you're feeling. You're allowed. That's what they're there for. They're not going to take you into care if you say you don't want to go. There are loads of things they can do to help you before they do that. Care's a last resort. Don't just struggle by yourself. If you use everybody you can use, you'll be much better able to cope. And your schooling won't suffer. Bet you've missed school more than you've been.' He lifted me down to the entrance to casualty. 'I'll stop nagging now, but please do as I say. They'll help you, I promise.'

I knew he wouldn't tell any social workers. My parents were doctors, so the normal processes didn't apply. An NHS worker who shopped a doctor to social work would be ostracised by his bosses. Maybe not now, in these enlightened times, but then, definitely. They kept my mother in overnight and let me stay in a small room next to her ward. I had fun with the nurses while she slept. She didn't need an operation. She always used to say she'd have given anything to take the pain I felt in my legs, that she'd rather suffer it than see me go through it. I realised that night how untrue that was, how the thought of surgery, however minor, filled her with real dread.

'What about my pills, Nic? Did you bring them with

you? Can you go and get them or ask your father to bring them in? What if they clash with the anaesthetic?'

She became more and more agitated. There were times when, if you tried to follow her thought patterns, you'd see why she drank; because of the terrifying chaos rattling around inside her head.

Once Jim had gone, Mummy decided to get out of bed and wander the corridors, shouting at other patients like a demented banshee, saying: 'Hello, I've been picked up for being drunk and disorderly, how about you?' accosting people in varying states of pain and illness. Once she got bored of this routine with strangers, she started on me.

'Get this child away from me,' she shouted at an old man who was waiting anxiously for somebody. She pointed at me, screeching as loudly as she could. 'That girl there, she's trying to poison me.'

Nobody seemed to know what to do, they didn't recognise her hallucinations and confusion for what they were. She had DTs from alcohol withdrawal. I'd seen her develop it before, most memorably when she'd visited my school. It took about forty-eight hours to reach its peak. I wondered when she'd last had a drink. Maybe drugs had caused her to fall down the stairs. Who knows?

Daddy was always telling us this was Edinburgh's main teaching hospital, yet, despite all the consultants and nurses on duty, the only person who knew my mother had DTs appeared to be me. Not that they wanted to know. They just wanted her to shut up.

'Sit the fuck down,' I heard a beefy nurse with massive calf muscles mutter under her breath.

'She's got DTs,' I ventured. 'Delirium tremens. I've seen her like this before, scared, seeing strange animals, talking rubbish for hours.'

The nurse looked appalled, whether at my mother's condition or the fact that I'd caught her swearing at a patient, I'll never know. I suspected the latter.

Nurse Beefy made a hasty exit and my mother lurched towards me, raising one hand as if to slap my face. A male nurse appeared, a young guy with glasses, a heavy frown and bright red spots on his chin, and grabbed her arm. She turned on him.

'This child has been trying to poison me!' she shouted.

Instead of reasoning with her, the young man edged her towards a row of empty chairs with worn seats, further down the corridor at a discreet distance from the other patients, and told her to sit on one of them. I followed them, grateful that someone had taken charge.

'I think I'll go home,' I lied, putting my jacket back on and winking at the spotty nurse.

'Yeah, good idea.' The nurse looked pleased at my quick thinking. 'Off you go and leave this poor woman alone.'

Our assurances seemed to calm her; at least long

enough for the bespectacled nurse to excuse himself for a minute, returning with what I assumed was a tranquilliser and a glass of water. I edged away from her towards the exit but stayed in the corridor, watching from a distance.

'What's that?' she asked, suspicious, pointing at the blue pill in the palm of his hand.

'It'll make you feel more relaxed,' the young man said. My mother's eyes, by now hooded and cold, were full of misery. She had an exhausted look on her face, huge bags under her eyes, as she turned on the young nurse for a second time. To my horror, she brought her hand up sharply beneath his with a slapping sound, sending the little pill flying into the distance. None of us saw it land.

'I'll get another one,' the lad said, with remarkable restraint.

'Don't bloody bother!' she bawled. 'I've had enough of you lot shutting me up when it suits you. I'm a doctor, you fool. Think I don't know a Valium when I see one? When I want pills, you won't give them to me. When I don't, you're ramming them down my throat, you contrary, bloody-minded, bloody morons.'

I looked at her. Nobody would ever guess how charming she was when she wasn't drunk or drying out. I began to wonder which was worse: her drunk and out of it or her sober with DTs.

'How about I find you a nice cup of tea?' the young nurse said to her gently. With this he struck lucky and she had the good grace to smile and sit down as I followed him down the corridor into what I thought was a cupboard with a sign on the door: Duty Room.

'I'm Brian,' he said. 'Look, have a seat, won't you. Would you like something to drink?'

I shook my head.

'That your mum?' Brian added.

'Yep. I'm Nicola.'

I sat down and looked at the table. It was littered with carry-out wrappers, juice cans, cigarette packets, trays of half-eaten Chinese, soggy chips, unwashed dishes covering every surface inch. It lay there, amassing more evidence daily, like a history of the Scottish takeaway trade – not a great advert for the health service.

'Excuse the mess,' Brian called from kettle duty. 'We never get time to clean up.'

'At least you don't have mice like we do,' I called back and he raised his eyebrows.

These nurses had probably saved my mother's life. There she was, out in the corridor, ranting, raving, surrounded by sick people yet still vying to be the centre of attention. She somehow always managed to have everybody running around after her.

'I'm going to try her again with this Valium.' Brian winked at me and left the room. I sat looking around the nurses' duty room, taking in each soiled wrapper and discarded container.

At times I wished my mother had nothing: no house, no money and no family. I wished she were on skid row where she'd have to come to her senses and do something for herself, sober up, in other words. With me and the family to take care of her, she was never going to make any effort to stop drinking. We were the cushion she could scream behind.

Brian came back in, looking pleased.

'She took it, agreed she was really anxious and could do with calming down. She actually said "thank you", which is more than most of them do.'

'Thanks,' I said weakly, sure she'd have held it under her tongue then spat it out the minute his back was turned. She loved taking pills but only those administered by her own hand. Mummy didn't like being told what to do.

'It must be awful working here,' I said, trying to make conversation.

'You see things,' Brian agreed. 'But I love it. It's much more interesting than working on the wards. Mind if I have a fag?'

'Go ahead.'

'We see a lot of people like your mum – the ones you don't really expect to find in a place like this.'

'Why not? D'you think she's too posh to be in here?' I said it too quickly, sounding defensive.

Brian wasn't embarrassed. 'I dunno.' He inhaled deeply on his cigarette and blew out a cloud of smoke, which filled the small room, made the air taste like a damp sock then hit the back of my throat so hard I started to cough.

Brian carried on talking: 'People like your mum usually manage to hide their drunkenness. They've got homes, beds to go to when they've overdone it. A lot of the drunks we get in here have lost all of that.

'They may have started out with a nice home,' he said, 'but, gradually, they're off, losing their friends, their family, their home and job. One minute you see them, drinking from a glass in the pub, the next it's from a bottle out in the street. It happens as quickly as that. They start out with everything, they end up with nothing. That's the way it goes. By the time they reach us, nobody wants to know them.'

I must have looked amazed.

'Sorry, have I said something I shouldn't?' he asked.

'No,' I replied. 'It's just that I was thinking exactly that a few minutes ago.'

Brian's lips smacked against his mug as he drank something smelling like strong coffee.

'Could I have a drink of juice?' I asked. He jumped up and opened a small refrigerator, took out a carton of fresh orange juice and poured it into a cup, after peering into it to check it was clean.

'Funny,' I said. 'If she didn't have us to clear up after her, she'd probably come to her senses more quickly. She'd be a lot better off.'

'They tend to take it out on us,' Brian added. 'I don't mean your mum. She wasn't bad. We see far worse, a lot of violence. I've been smacked in the mouth a few times, by women as well as men.'

His coffee finished, fag stubbed out, he led the way back to my mother. She was sitting head thrown back, snoring quietly. Maybe she'd swallowed the pill after all. I sat down beside her and held her hand.

Brian kept coming back to check up on us, like a cat stalking a wounded bird.

'We're okay,' I said. 'I'm used to looking after her, honest.'

'You are an amazing girl,' he replied. 'Have you ever thought of becoming a nurse when you grow up?'

'I grew up a long time ago,' I muttered. 'And I've been a nurse for as long as I can remember.'

After that hospital visit, Mummy agreed to try AA. Even though it wasn't for her, she met people there who tried hard to help her, phoned her over the years despite the fact she never stopping drinking for very long. I went with her the first time. We climbed a grotty tenement stair right in the centre of Edinburgh, its entrance littered with crushed cans; empty crisp packets swirling in a mild wind. We rang a bell, a door swung open and a young man took my mother's hand and shook it firmly. He nodded at some others who came in behind us. Judging by the way they reacted to us, we were the only newcomers.

A middle-aged man stood at the front of the room, chewing his nails, an activity totally at odds with his suave appearance. He went to sit down in front of an audience of empty chairs.

'I'm Bob,' he said, beckoning us to a table where he pointed out the coffee and biscuits. He chatted away about himself, told us he'd been sober for four years and felt the best he'd done in his entire adult life. By this time, Mummy was taking deep breaths in an attempt to calm herself down.

We sat near the back, next to a woman with long, straggly, grey hair who smiled warmly and whispered something which sounded like 'Bob's sharing.'

His story turned out to be graphic in its repulsive detail.

'All I have to do,' he said, 'is stay away from that first drink one day at a time. That's because I know the next one I take will come in a great big bucket. The truth is I was a different person in drink. There are things I did, people I upset. I'm going to share one or two of them with you. At one time, when I was drinking a whole bottle of whisky first thing in the morning, I was suffering terrible mood swings. I was at home alone and my wife was at work. She was keeping us because I'd lost my job and gambled or drunk away all our savings. We were penniless and in debt. That day, I was at home with our terrier, Bramble. I was drinking through in the kitchen, sitting at the table, mulling over my problems, a real case of "poor me", while Bramble was yapping at people going past the window. She was a wee hairy bundle, a wonderful, affectionate pup. She adored me, followed me everywhere. But Bramble often barked and, when I'd been drinking, the barking got on my nerves.

'That day, I'd shouted at her a few times but it didn't make any difference. After putting up with her racket for half an hour or so, I went through, and, in a split second, I picked her up by her front paws and flung her against the wall – and did it with as much strength as I could muster. I'm 6ft 2ins and hefty. The first time I threw her, I must have broken every bone in her body. All I heard was a stifled cry, like wind being violently squeezed out of sails. Then her wee body went limp. But that wasn't enough for me, oh no, I had to keep the punishment going, keep thrashing that wee furry body against the wall, like a man possessed, until she was in pieces. When I realised I'd killed her, my rage gave way to terror and, eventually, to a sort of remorse. What had I done? How could I ever tell my wife what I'd done to her precious dog?'

I was aghast, horrified. This was better than the cinema. My mother was looking alarmed, not at all as if she were identifying with anyone. An elderly woman, scarf wrapped round her head, stood up, sending her wooden chair flying backwards until it toppled into the lap of the man behind. She glared at Bob before marching through the door, leaving it to swing noisily backwards and forwards. Bob stared at the floor. Nobody moved.

'I began to panic,' he continued. 'I had an hour until my wife was due home but I was drunk, though rapidly sobering up, it has to be said.' He stopped and looked round for effect. 'I wrapped the remaining bits of Bramble inside an old blanket, put the bundle into a black sack and went out, carrying the dog under my arm. I swayed up the street, through the main shopping area and out of the town until I came to the woods where I dug a hole with my hands and buried the bag, feeling worse than ever.

'I couldn't face going home so I stopped off at a pub and drank several pints with whisky chasers, just to make sure I felt in charge again. I was so drunk by then I had no idea what happened next but I must have got into a fight. I was picked up by the police and woke up, in the middle of the night, in a cell. They phoned Melissa, who came to get me. When she arrived, the first thing she asked was where the dog was.'

I noticed sweat running down Bob's face. I sneaked a look at Mummy. She wasn't shaking as much and was watching Bob, her lower lip trembling.

'I'd been through many different scenarios in my head,' Bob went on. 'I had even considered denying all knowledge of Bramble's disappearance but, somehow, guilt and the lack of drink were getting the better of me. In the end, I said Bramble had been run over while we were out having our walk and, although Melissa knew I hardly ever took Bramble out, she seemed to accept this. I was so relieved. We drove home in silence, her with tears running down her face the whole way.

'By this time, I was scarily sober, shaking violently, only just able to stop myself from retching. My wife parked in the driveway, we got out and went into the house.

'What's that, Bob?' she said, pointing at some streaks of blood smeared across the living-room wall. I could see Bramble's hair everywhere, on the settee, on the wall, bits of flesh scattered over the beige carpet. I couldn't speak. It was guilt and shame mixed together. I couldn't bear to tell my wife, tell anyone, what I'd done. I knelt down in front of her and wept, begged her to forgive me. I don't know how long I stayed like that, on my knees but that was it, my personal gutter.'

Bob stopped and took a sip of water from a glass on the table in front of him, next to his copy of the Big Book, the AA bible. First published in 1939, it tells the stories of men and women who have overcome alcoholism and sets out the twelve steps of recovery.

With a slight crack in his voice, Bob said: 'Despite being devastated at what had happened to the dog, and after refusing to speak to me for several days, my wife agreed to give me one more chance, having already given me umpteen. I suppose Melissa knew it could have been her hitting that wall instead of our poor pup. She said if I went to AA, stuck to the programme and accepted the help, she'd stay with me. Not otherwise. So, I did and it was pure hell: the cold turkey, the temptations, facing all the things I'd done, dropping all my old drinking cronies who couldn't accept that I'd stopped. It would have been oh-so-easy to go back, but that was four years ago and I'm still here.'

There was a burst of applause. Everyone, except me, was clapping – even my mother. I couldn't, I just kept thinking about Bramble and hating Bob for what he had done to her.

'Melissa is here tonight,' Bob added. He pointed and we all turned to look at a tanned woman, beaming from the back row. 'And, at home we have another dog, a Labrador called Sam. He's five, every bit as cute as the last one – except Melissa's the leader of the pack now, for Sam and for me.

'Best of all is I've earned my wife's trust and respect. She still goes out to work, and now so do I. We tend to work at different times and, this is what's so hard for me to take in, my wife actually trusts me with our dog.' Bob's voice faltered. He took a deep breath and continued, his voice rising and falling with emotion. 'That's what's so great about this programme. She lets me take Sam out for walks. She even leaves me alone in the house with him.'

There was a slight commotion at the back of the hall and a man piped up: 'Bet the wee bastard knows no tae bark though.'

Everybody turned to look. Somebody had obviously been drinking, against the rules of the Fellowship. Another man stood up and signalled to the wee guy to leave, which he did reluctantly, all the while still laughing at his own joke. He walked unsteadily to the back of the hall, chuckling loudly.

'That's what AA did for me,' Bob continued, ignoring the disturbance. 'It gave me back my life. If that sounds like an exaggeration, it isn't. In fact, it's probably an understatement.'

When they asked Mummy if she wanted to say anything, she said no at first, then yes. She stood up, still shaking, opened and closed her mouth but no words came. She stuttered and managed to say: 'My name's Monica, I'm an alcoholic.'

The group all clapped, one or two stood up and cheered.

Although she relished their support, AA didn't really work for her. She hated the macho drinking stories the men told and thought the atmosphere was too competitive, like some mysterious hierarchy of sin. That first visit she wanted to leave straight away, not even stay for coffee, and we made our way discreetly to the door. She did stay in touch with certain people from the Fellowship through her life but never really gave the programme a chance.

'The next time I take a drink, it'll be in a great big bucket,' I heard Bob say again as I closed the door. I winced at the pat expression, buttoned up my coat, pulled my collar up around my ears for warmth, and went downstairs into the street. I know my mother went back to the occasional AA meeting, dipping in and out of it as the mood took her, but she never again asked me to go with her.

# Chapter 10

# *Like Mother, Like Daughter*

My A-level results were exactly what St Andrews University had asked for. But when I left school, I couldn't face it. The thought of having to mix with people my own age and be sociable terrified me. School had been so sheltered, so easy by comparison to the prospect of university. There, we prayed all the time, didn't go out with boys, didn't go out at all. I was happy hiding away. The other girls in my class couldn't wait to leave and lead a normal life. I would have happily remained cloistered with the nuns for the rest of my days. With this character trait obvious to all who knew me, Sister Clemont, the matron as well as a good friend, asked if I'd like to spend a year at the Mother House in the south of France. I could teach, she said, and find out whether I really had a vocation. I was convinced I did, at that time. Becoming a nun appealed to me as a way out of facing up to a world I knew very little about.

I had to write to St Andrews and say I wanted to take a gap year. They agreed. My parents didn't care one way or the other. They were surprised I'd passed my A levels, never mind got the entrance qualifications necessary for university. I wasn't surprised, though. I had worked every day, sometimes all night, to pass.

The day I left for France, I took a taxi to the airport as my parents didn't have time to see me off. My father thought the idea of me becoming a nun was hilarious. As a Catholic, he might have been proud, but wasn't. He was proud of Richard because he was doing medicine at Guy's Hospital in London. I was the family black sheep, a loser in his eyes, always had been. Becoming a nun was an oh-so-appropriate way for me to go. He smirked whenever he mentioned it.

The Mother House, Le Couvent de la Sainte Famille, gave me a nasty shock in terms of discovering who I was. I taught English to French kids, most of them about my own age. I started buying vodka from a shop in the small village where I was staying. I drank alone in my room and felt incredibly isolated and unsettled, needing a drink to face the large classes of children. In time, I developed a crush on a male teacher who worked in the school, and gradually I swapped my devotion to genuflecting and attending Mass for obsessing about him, trying to bump into him in the school grounds. At that time, my French was almost fluent. I could have studied the language at university but, increasingly, I wanted to hide away in the safety of the bottle.

By the time I returned to Edinburgh a year later, I was drinking a lot, usually in secret, just like my mother. At least I thought people didn't know I drank, but they must have done. Instead of resuming life at home, I rented a flat with a lot of charm that lay between the purple rinses of Morningside and the armchair socialists of Bruntsfield. It was painted white throughout, with lots of candles in alcoves, Berber twist carpets and Turkish rugs. The best thing about it was that my parents, and their attendant problems, weren't living with me. I soon realised that living alone was how I functioned best. I never felt lonely. When the pressure was off, when I didn't have to socialise or compete or perform, I existed in a state of permanent relief. There was nobody shouting, nobody to look after, nobody to impress.

I worked at odd jobs in the city, as a receptionist, filling in time before university. I still went home a lot, once a week at least, to see my mother and check she was still alive. They had moved southwest, to the other end of Edinburgh. They had sold our home in Murrayfield for a pittance because of the decay caused by twenty years of neglect.

Ten or so years later, I stopped my car at the postbox outside the front gate of our old house, walked past the huge holly bush, just as it was bearing its berries, and rang the bell to ask the new inhabitants if I could have a look around. Foolish, but I wanted to know whether it had really been that bad. They let me in.

The house was all different colours, bright, beautifully decorated. The sight of the back garden, the memories of all those dead pets and of the berry fights with my brothers, stirred such a feeling of nostalgia inside me that I could barely breathe.

But despite the brightness of the house in its present state, I could still see through the years to the old dark patches on the paintwork, smell the mix of gin and drugs, see chips in all the wood, feel the worn, stained carpets beneath my feet. But, most vivid of all, in one of the bedrooms, I could see my mother lying on her old bed, lit cigarette in one hand, eyes cold, distant, empty; ashtray piled high with butts on her bedside table; her body moving only to reach for another drink from a bottle under the bed.

This was a family home, now. All those years of pain, cobwebs and discarded bottles banished by a few licks of paint. They were history. We were history.

The woman showing me round took me up the back stairs to the attic and threw open the door. 'There,' she announced with pride, 'we never painted this room so that we could tell people this was how the Barrys left it.'

I had told her I was a Barry. She didn't seem an unkind

woman, just angry at the state we'd left the house in. As a family, we managed to offend certain people, to rub against their sensibilities, unsettle their peace.

After I left, I walked down the hill and round the block, up the lane behind our house to the back garden, where I gently pushed the gate until it creaked open. The walls separating our house from the neighbours' seemed a lot lower than they had in my childhood. The pink gravel was the same but the pigeon hut had gone. I looked up at the high windows. All I could see was myself as a child, looking out, praying for it all to end.

No wonder I loved having my own home.

I set out to see my mother one morning. The boys were all away: Michael busy working in the theatre in England, Peter living with his wife, Lindsay, and family in Australia and Richard had a job in a London hospital. Boys never bother looking after their parents, not when they have sisters to do it for them. My carer role wasn't a noble one, though. I used looking after my mother to excuse myself from having to live life to the full. I didn't have boyfriends because I was too busy looking after her. I barely had friends, just kept myself to myself, and drank, usually alone. Just like her.

I felt strange: sick, weak, very shaky. I'd had so much to drink the night before. I sat down at the back of the bus as it bounced southwards, holding my breath, hoping the nausea would pass. Instead, it got worse. I couldn't be sick on a bus, no way. Then it was out before I could stop it, a horrible, pinkish pool on the red seat beside me. I couldn't believe it. Here I was, travelling on a bus in Edinburgh, throwing up like . . . like what? An alcoholic. I knew I needed a drink, knew I had to lift this feeling of wretchedness. It was becoming increasingly common, this desire to escape, to feel different, more confident.

My self-esteem was not improving with the passing years. In that sense, at least, I was turning into my mother. I didn't know whether I was an alcoholic according to any textbook definition. I never physically craved the stuff, unlike a lot of people. I never actually liked drink very much. My habit was 'performance related', as they say in business. When I had to mix, I drank. I was a perfectionist, always wanted to be better, more accomplished, to be liked – all the time behaving in a way that invited hostility. I certainly had a problem with drink. After all, normal people didn't *need* a drink, and they didn't throw up when they took a drink. I did.

Checking to see whether anyone had noticed, I stood up and changed seats, moving to the front just behind the driver, a fat bloke with a cigarette behind his ear. When he looked up at his mirror and caught my eye, I shrugged and stared out the window at the crowds milling around the shops. My stomach ached, badly. Perhaps I was hungry, but the thought of eating made me want to gag again. I took a few deep breaths and watched a woman trying to push a pram through a rotating shop door.

If only I could remember what had happened last night with that guy I'd picked up in the pub; hopefully nothing. I didn't often go to pubs but, when I did, I never remembered coming back out. Sean, I think the last one was called. Exactly a week ago, I awoke, naked, in a king-sized bed, in a room painted bright red, with a can of extra strong lager by my side and a ticking clock on the mantelpiece. I hated ticking clocks, so immediately knew I wasn't at home. I lay there; don't know how long for, trying to remember the night before. Sean was the builder who'd been buying me drinks in the Abbotsford Bar. I sneakily looked at the chair over by the window where a bundle of men's clothes lay in a heap. Sean's presumably. He had a thin, sullen face and a mass of red hair. He was snoring so loud it sounded as if a farm tractor had been crossing the floor for the past fifteen minutes.

Could I get up, dress and leave without waking him? Besides, I wanted to be sick. I wasn't going to do that in front of some bloke I hardly knew, I'd picked up in the pub. How could I have spent the night with a stranger, again? Drink made it so easy. It didn't matter whether they were married or single. Nothing mattered through a haze of booze; but waking the next morning brought a horror all of its own. I never gave myself a chance to get to know a man. Sex wouldn't be so bad if love were involved, although I felt that my desire for affection made love sound like some sort of moral disinfectant.

I tried to concentrate on the road. The bus was a mile or so from my stop and I wanted fresh air. Struggling to my feet, I strode to the door, hanging onto the metal bar above for dear life. I looked back at my original seat. The sick couldn't be seen from the door. I hoped nobody sat in it without realising.

I got off a stop before my parents' home where there was an off-licence, walked into the shop and pretended to look through the red wines. It was so quiet. There was a musty scent, a combination of dust and alcohol. A bespectacled young man stood behind the counter, peering at me studying the bottles of wine. I was gearing myself up to asking for spirits. Their effect was almost instant whereas wine took time. Eventually, I turned to face the man in the glasses.

'Could I have half a bottle of vodka?'

'Sure,' he replied, grabbing half a bottle of Smirnoff from a shelf behind him. 'Anything else?'

'No thanks, that's all.'

I left the shop, relieved he hadn't seemed to make any assumptions. I was paranoid about people thinking I had a drink problem. I clutched the bottle in my right pocket. I walked for a half a mile, heading south, before turning into a public loo close to my parents' house.

The loo looked as if a typhoon had swept through it

just before I arrived: graffiti all over the walls, outside as well as in; no soap at the sinks, no hand towels and the drier was out of order. The place smelt like a full nappy that had been left lying for a week. I tiptoed into one of the cubicles, noticed the floor was soaking wet, hung my bag on a convenient hook and tried to lock the door, which kept swinging open. I held one foot against it, while fishing the bottle out of my coat pocket, and sat down, careful to place my free hand between my skin and the seat, for hygiene's sake.

Although I hated vodka, loathed the way it hit the back of my throat leaving a faint taste of burnt cardboard, I loved the instant boost it gave, the warm feeling that filled me with the confidence I so craved. I took a long swig and swallowed the harsh liquid. Nausea hit me again and I clutched my stomach, trying not to be sick – I couldn't possibly waste the effect so soon. There was no way I was going back into that off-licence to buy more.

I looked around me, my eyes lighting on a can of cider some woman had pushed into a corner behind the cistern. Someone had been here before me. I despised myself for being weak, but the exercise in self-loathing never lasted very long. Within minutes, I began to feel better, my earlier sickness completely forgotten. Stuffing the bottle back inside my pocket, I opened the door and went to wash my hands at the dirty sink. In the mirror my cheeks beamed back at me, a ruddy pink. I grinned at myself, testing out the fake smile I needed to give my mother.

Walking past the row of local shops, a new spring in my step, I popped into the newsagent's and bought some strong mints to disguise my breath. Approaching the house, I reached into my handbag for the spare key I always kept zipped in a side pocket, placed it in the lock and opened the door. The house was eerily still, invariably a bad sign. I climbed the stairs and stood on the landing, looking around for signs of life.

'Mummy. It's me.'

Deciding she must be asleep, I went to the sitting room and sat down. Straightaway, I noticed it wasn't as clean as I'd left it the last time I visited a week earlier. There were cobwebs on the ceiling and dust on the small fireside table, although my old chair was in exactly the same position.

Suddenly, I was aware of the body stretched out on the kitchen floor. Even though I knew straightaway it was my mother, I approached warily, preparing myself in a detached way, for the discovery that, this time, she'd definitely be dead. This wasn't wishful thinking, just a fear that had been there as long as I could remember. People who behaved like she did fell over, hurt themselves and died. It was expected. I had grown used to this heart-in-mouth feeling that, one day, one accident too many, she might be dead. But I never really believed it would happen.

My mother was lying face down, totally still. Undeterred, I knelt down on the tiles, noticing – despite the emergency – how greasy they were and, with difficulty, because she was heavy, rolled her over so that she lay on her back. At this point I realised that, although practically unconscious with drink, she was breathing. I ran to the sink and picked up a cold, wet cloth, brought it back and dabbed her forehead until she tried to open her eyes and shake herself out of her drunkenness.

'Mummy, get up, Daddy will be back soon!' I shouted the usual threat, despite being sure he was away. She glared at me, slightly bewildered by my presence. I lifted her head only to watch it flop back down on the floor.

'What the hell have you been drinking?' I bellowed, grabbing her hand to try and rouse her. She glared at me again, then closed her eyes.

'What's going on?' I said.

Her fingers tightened around my hand. She was pulling me towards her while pushing herself up with her other hand, trying to focus.

'What the hell have you been drinking?' I asked again, glaring back at her.

'No, wait at minute,' she retorted very slowly. 'What the hell have *you* been drinking?'

*

I'd managed to drag my mother through to her bedroom and remove her clothes without my customary feeling of rage. I never meant to stay at home for the night but a slowly developing hangover had got the better of me and I fell asleep on my bed when I'd really meant only to snooze. As a child, I used to lie in the dark listening out for my mother, unable to sleep for worrying. Would she stumble and fall during the night? Then, when she did fall, would she be drunk or dead? Nothing much had changed except that, last night, fifteen or so years after my mother had replaced social drinking with alcoholism, there were two drunks in the house.

I started humming as I'd always done in childhood, hoping to drown out the sound of my mother calling, tapping an accompaniment to my tunes with my fingers under the sheet. I'd hear my name and hum even louder, only to leap out of bed when she called. My sleep was drink-induced, one reason why the dawn came up like thunder the next day. My mother wasn't making a sound this morning. Fishy. I guessed she must have had more to drink during the night, otherwise she'd have been up pestering me to go out and buy some. It drove me mad when she did that.

I went downstairs and started doing what looked like a week's washing up. There were plates and cups piled high in the sink, carry-out cartons scattered all over the table and floor. I washed the dishes and laid them out to drain in the sun streaming through the kitchen window.

'Nicola,' the voice came from upstairs, her bedroom.

'Yes.' I hadn't meant to sound so surly.

'I'd kill for a cup of tea.'

I switched on the kettle, searched in the cupboards for teabags and then found some foul-smelling milk in the fridge. I poured it down the sink, put two mugs on a tray and waited for the kettle to boil. We'd have it black.

My mother's room was still in darkness except for a small bedside lamp by her bed. She lay, curled up, facing the window, her back to the door. This room was similar to her bedroom in Murrayfield, but more prison-cell-like and without the stately Victorian ceilings. There were one or two chipped antiques on the chest of drawers she hadn't managed to sell and the walls looked as if someone had carried out a dirty protest over them. The bedding smelled and the air was thick with tobacco smoke. She had kept the old laundry basket, full to the brim with empty bottles. Her former bedroom had seemed a part of the house. This one didn't. It felt like an isolation ward. She lay in bed all day drinking and smoking, her face expressionless, occasionally watching the small black-and-white TV on a chest of drawers opposite the door. And it was so dark you couldn't see unless the light was on.

I put the tray down at the end of her bed and went to

draw the curtains. Mummy made an effort to sit up, her shoulders slumped forward, a frown on her face.

'No milk?'

'It's off,' I muttered.

'I meant to get some more yesterday,' she explained, 'but didn't make it to the shops in the end.'

Did she really expect me to be cheerful and friendly, not even to mention her performance the previous night? Her avoidance tactics bugged me.

'You gave me a fright last night,' I started.

'I wasn't expecting you,' was all she said.

'Mummy . . .'

'Okay, I'm sorry. But, you're so like your father. You never ask how I am or what I've been doing. It's always how much have I been drinking and why.' She was sorry for her behaviour, I could tell, but angry, as well, at having been caught.

'That's probably true,' I said, feeling my cheeks start to burn. 'So, I come home and find my mother out cold on the kitchen floor and I'm expected to say: "Hi, how're you? Been doing anything interesting lately?"'

My mother, now in her late fifties and despite her years of drinking, managed to look elegant occasionally. She had neat greyish-black hair swept back off her face and large brown eyes, somewhat red-rimmed of late. Her chin was beginning to slacken, her mouth to tremble, and lipstick, always applied in the morning, had smeared around her mouth by lunchtime. Her breasts and stomach sagged, her shoulders seemed to cave in when she stood up. She was smiling at me, her frown evaporating slowly. She took a sip of tea. I noticed her hands, covered in liver spots, were shaking so much the cup clattered against the saucer, spilling tea this way and that. She sat huddled up in bed like a little old woman. How long could she go on like this? I looked at her sheets, couldn't help it. My eyes were drawn to the stains up near the pillow – drool, booze she'd spilt. It was disgusting.

'There must have been so many times you've come into the house and found me in that state and been disappointed, angry . . . hated me even,' she said. 'A kid coming home, wanting her tea, wanting to chat about her day and all she finds to greet her is a drunk mother.'

A statement or a question, I wasn't sure which. Anyway, what was the point of asking me now, when it was too late? She wasn't looking at me, but keeping her head down. If she had looked up, seen how upset I was, we might have discovered something approaching the truth.

I drank my tea, grimacing at the lack of milk. At last we looked at each other, but the moment had passed. I wasn't going to deny I'd hated her or been angry. After all, those memories she evoked still had the power to waken me in the middle of the night: all those years spent hurrying home from school, never knowing how she would be. Would she be wandering about, anxious, bright red in the face, desperate for some more booze; or would she be that placid way, when she'd had just enough drink to calm her down but not enough to knock her out; or, would she be unconscious on the bed?

'Let's start again,' Mummy started to say. 'I'll stop. I promise I'll stop.'

'Forget it. We've been through all that so many times. Let's just take it a day at a time.'

'God, you do sound pious, Nic.'

The remark stung. It was meant to. I had been trying to take her seriously, trying to offer support. It hadn't worked. Nothing ever worked with her; not taking her drink away or diluting it with water; not AA, no matter how hard the members of that organisation tried. They did help me, when I went to Alateen, a group for young people, family members of alcoholics. The most important lesson I learned from them was to stand back and let my mother get on with it, stop trying to work out ways of stopping her drinking, that you can't change or control your parents but you can detach from their problems while continuing to love them. They told me that for every alcoholic there were at least five people affected by their behaviour.

'Where's Daddy?' I said, changing the subject.

'He's at some conference in England. He's probably having an affair.'

'Mummy, that's ridiculous,' I snapped.

'Why? He's an attractive man,' she paused, adding waspishly, 'if you like that sort of thing.' She smirked. 'Women do seem to like him though. He's got a good job, a wife who fails to satisfy him. He's got every reason to stray.'

'What about you?' I wondered out loud.

'Me? Have an affair? Who the hell with? These days, I hardly ever leave my bedroom, never mind have affairs. Anyway, I reckon it must have healed up by now.'

'Mummy! A lover might give you reason to stop . . .'

'To what, darling? Have a makeover? Do something about my fashion sense?'

She knew what I'd been going to say. She didn't like – no, she couldn't stand me nagging her about her drinking, mainly because she had no intention of doing anything about the problem.

'You need to get out of the house. It's beyond a joke now. You never leave this room.'

'I miss you, darling,' she said suddenly. 'We used to have such good times . . . some of the time anyway.' This was said with so much uncertainty – as if she was sure I'd respond with a sarcastic comment. I nodded in agreement.

'There's no one to talk to, no one to laugh with. When Claude is here, which is hardly ever these days, he never speaks, just sits in his room. It's so lonely.'

'Mummy, he never spoke. That's nothing new. What happened to that bloke who used to come round at night sometimes, when Daddy was working at the hospital? You liked him, didn't you?'

'Oh God, he was awful. I met him at the Crichton. Mike. He was an outpatient for years. He used to come and chat to us inpatients. I fell for him, I suppose. The last I heard he had been arrested for vagrancy. He was an alcoholic. Your father met him at the Crichton once and loathed him on sight, said he was disgusting. Mike had been in the army and was a gent, fallen on hard times. I wasn't so miserable when he came round. He was just a friend, though,' she added, rather primly.

'Why don't you leave Daddy if you feel like that?'

For once her expression looked genuine: 'I don't know if I've got the nerve to make it on my own.'

'Without Daddy? Or without the bottle?'

She gave me a withering look but, for once, didn't get angry at my mention of drink. She screwed up her face, considered my question.

'I know you won't believe me, darling, but I have tried to stop. I used to think I could stop anytime I wanted. Now I'm not so sure.'

'Christ, Mummy, you didn't even stop when you had me.' I could have bitten my tongue off. We'd been chatting away so affably then I'd ruined it. Her silence filled me with fear. I became aware of feeling sick and slightly giddy. I'd gone too far and just when we'd been getting on so well, just when I thought I'd found some kind of connection between us. Typical. I had to blunder in with my size sixteens.

It was the first time I'd ever brought up the subject of her drinking while pregnant; a subject so taboo that my parents never even talked about it. She lay back down as tears rolled down her face, visible, just, in the darkness, soaking her grubby pillow. The large orange-and-white-patterned box of Coty face powder sat on the table beside her. I could see bits of the loose powder caked on her cheeks, smeared now by tears.

'Mummy, I'm sorry.' I put out my hand to take hers but she ignored it.

'I think you all forget how ill I was when I had you,' she said, resentment in her tone. 'I had a retrocecal appendix just as you were due. When the surgeon told me that one of us could die, I told him I didn't care if I lost my baby. The pain was too bad.'

My mother could be incredibly insensitive. She was forever telling Peter how, shortly after he was born, she had gone out one evening, stood on a bridge over the Thames, lifted him out of his pram and prepared to throw him into the river. She said a passer-by had stopped her just in time. The reason she couldn't cope with her baby was that, while she was pregnant, her favourite sibling, also called Peter, had been killed in Burma. His body was flown back to England and he was buried alongside his father, Sir Maurice Craig, in a village churchyard in Sussex. Her brother had been trying to save the lives of fellow members of his squadron by removing a grenade from their tent. He died a hero and she called her middle son Peter as a tribute to her dead brother.

Mummy had stopped crying. 'Maybe a good cry would do you good,' I suggested. 'You always seem to bottle things up.'

We both smiled, appreciating the unintentional pun. We looked at each other for a few moments. She didn't start crying again and, for the first time in years, I felt a sense of real intimacy between us and leaned forward to give her a peck on the cheek.

'If I could just have a drink . . .' she muttered, for once having the decency to sound slightly embarrassed.

I wanted to throw my tea at her. Just as I thought we'd established a connection, she shattered it by reverting back to her old ways. I slammed my cup down on the bedside table. It was as if she took you so far, assuring you things were going to get better, and then, suddenly, she'd shatter any faith you'd ever had in her.

'Darling, I'm sorry. It's just that I'm not quite ready, can't stop just like that, you know. In a couple of days, I'll have another go.'

'Another go?' I stood up, looked at her with distaste –

pity mingled with contempt – and flounced out of the room, standing for a few minutes on the landing to compose myself.

'Nic, take the money out of my bag and pop out for a bottle of gin. Please, darling. I've run out.'

When I didn't answer, she said, 'Unless you've got some vodka left from your visit yesterday?' It was a killer line, delivered in a surprisingly cold, manipulative tone.

I went downstairs to dial the hospital. 'Can you page Dr Barry, please?' It was five minutes before they could trace my father, who was napping in his room.

'Hi, it's me,' I said.

He sounded busy. He had a good life in many respects, earned a lot of money. Occasionally he passed some of it my way, and was still in the habit of slipping me some at weekends when he wanted me to stay with Mummy while he went off climbing. She had used most of her savings and he kept his to himself. I can't remember him ever buying her any presents, not in the last decade of their marriage.

There was no way he was going to leave the hospital and come home now, just in case she had another drink, he told me. My father's aloofness was particularly difficult to deal with at times like these, when I longed for someone to listen, to be able to say: 'Daddy, can you help, please?' instead of always coming up against this armour-plated cool. He started mumbling something about appointments, making excuses. I said I had to go back home.

'Your mother'll be fine,' was all he would say.

I felt angry. I always did when I spoke to him. She wouldn't be fine and he knew it. It was almost as if he hoped she might come to some harm when there was no one there to smooth things over. Perhaps he *did* hope to come home and find her dead. How much easier his life would be as a result.

'Okay,' I said, anxious to end the conversation. 'See you sometime, maybe next week, if you have a minute. Okay, see you soon.' I sighed and replaced the receiver, went through to the sitting room, collapsed into my squishy armchair and listened to the rain outside. It was a wild day, the strong gale making the trees bend and sway. I closed my eyes, again hearing the sound of the wind in the garden.

I must have dozed off. Half an hour later, I heard Mummy stumble from her room, lurch across the landing towards the dining room and try to open the door, twisting the knob backwards and forwards, finally jerking it open in a fit of temper. She went through to the kitchen, opened the fridge door, closed it, fell against the sideboard then staggered back to her room and closed the door. She must have found something to drink.

\*

My father had been particularly cold towards me recently, the result of two drink-driving episodes in different cities in the same week. I will never forget the first time. It happened one evening when I was nineteen, after I'd borrowed his car. I was driving in the centre of Edinburgh, erratically. I dropped a cigarette and felt its heat on my thigh. I jumped, the car swerved and I was stopped. Drunk driving was not viewed in the same light then as it is today but it was still serious. I was too far gone to care at that stage.

I remember a police officer saying, 'Get out of the car, Miss. You're under arrest.' He looked angry, as if he considered himself personally responsible for my drunkenness. He was in his thirties, small, stocky, brusque.

'I didn't mean to swerve, officer,' I said, pronouncing every word with care. 'I sat on my cigarette and burnt myself in an unmentionable place.'

'Get out of the car,' he repeated, not a 'please' or a 'would you mind' – just 'Get out of the car. Anything you say will be taken down as evidence.'

He took out a notebook and pencil.

How many vodkas had I had? God knows. Twenty? I'd been celebrating a pal's birthday; not a real friend, just one of an ever-expanding crowd I mixed with in those days, people who lived to drink. I'd reached a point where no matter how much I drank, I could no longer achieve the same high. I always wanted more and often forgot what I'd been doing.

I tried to focus on the policeman. I knew the minute I stood up I'd give the game away that I was as pissed as a rat. I carefully opened the door and tried to struggle to my feet, thrust my whole body forward in an attempt to get out of the car but was barred by the officer who reached over and unhooked my seat belt. A young woman, displaying the irritating fervour of a trainee, stood by his side: short, fat, smug.

'Blow into this,' she said, shoving something with a tube under my nose. I took the contraption out of her hand, held it up to my lips and prepared to inhale. The policewoman was busily watching the dial. 'Blow now,' she said.

I breathed into it, a feeling of dread rising up inside me. I was holding back as much air as I could. All I could think about was that I'd been in my father's car. I could already hear his reaction. The trainee was obviously pleased with the result.

'Right, get into the back of the car,' she said, while the other officer grabbed my arm to stop me getting into the back of my own car.

'The back of the *police* car,' she said, raising her eyes to the heavens.

'Where are we going?' I asked.

The harder I tried to speak normally, the more my

words seemed to collide with each other on their way out of my mouth. They didn't answer. Once in the police car, I sank back into one of the rear seats, trying to disappear into upholstery that smelled of stale vomit and vinyl. The police couple sat in front, him driving, her staring straight ahead, both poker-faced. I guessed we were going to the police station. I must have dozed off; no idea how long for, but, when I came to, they were holding the car door open for me to get out. We went into a small room, which reeked of cigarette smoke, where they discussed phoning my father.

'Please don't,' I begged. 'You don't know what he's like, he'll . . .'

'You should have thought of that before,' chipped in the policewoman. 'It's his car you were driving. He has a right to know.'

I sat down, praying he wouldn't be at home. He'd be so angry. He was always angry these days. Once it had been with my mother and her drinking, but now he yelled at me as well. Listening to the conversation, I began to feel sick, and not because of the amount I'd had to drink, either.

'I suggest you calm down, Sir,' I heard the policeman say to my father. 'Your car's perfectly okay. Your daughter's fine as well, by the way.' Daddy obviously hadn't bothered to ask how I was. The officer paused to listen. 'No, no, we can bring her to you. It's not a problem, Sir.'

When he put the phone down, he turned to me and winked. 'Better get you a cup of coffee before you go home to face that.'

The policeman made me a large mug of black coffee. 'No milk,' he said, seeing me screw up my face. 'Get that down you. It's the best thing.'

I sipped the coffee and winced, at the temperature not the taste. My head was spinning. I felt so dizzy I wanted to retch. Instead I burst into tears.

'Bit of a temper, your dad?' the policeman said.

'A bit,' I repeated, nodding. It looked as if he was on my side after all. He spoiled it by asking: 'So, how long have you had a problem with drink?'

I stared at him blankly as something rushed to my head – blood or rage, I wasn't sure which. There were three chairs in the police interview room, a table covered in graffiti and a few scattered ashtrays piled high with discarded butts. There was no window. It was stifling.

'I haven't got a bloody problem with drink,' I bawled. 'It's my mother. She's the one with the problem.'

I jumped to my feet and paced around the room, well, tried to pace, but I was too unsteady and sat back down again to take another gulp of coffee. My face was bright scarlet, my breathing fast. He'd struck a nerve, but why? I wasn't the family alkie, she was. So, why was I so upset?

'You haven't got a problem with drink?' the officer repeated then turned to mutter to an older sergeant standing in the doorway. They both started laughing. The officer was shaking his head.

'I don't believe what I'm hearing,' he said. 'I know a lot of alcoholics have a problem with denial; they're always the last to see they have a problem, but this is ridiculous. Listen, young lady, anyone who dares take the wheel of a car when they're three times over the limit, then tells people they don't have a problem with drink, has a serious problem somewhere along the line. For God's sake, girl, think about it.' His face had turned as red as mine felt. 'And, if no one else has said you have a problem, it's because they're too scared.'

With that he stood up and the two men swept out of the interview room, slamming the door hard behind them. I could hear them out in the corridor, laughing. I stopped crying, felt too angry to cry. I knew what a drink problem was – something I didn't have. I had friends. I liked to go out and have a good time. Once in a while, I went too far. Who didn't? I wasn't like my mother, sneaking round the house, hiding bottles here, there and everywhere, drinking first thing in the morning and last thing at night. She couldn't function without it. She didn't wash properly, forgot to eat and look after herself. There was no comparison between her and me. It was half an hour before the door opened again. The woman was back, brandishing car keys.

'Come to take you home,' she said.

I picked up my bag and followed. We drove home in silence. By this time, I had sobered up, almost. A second officer followed us, driving my father's car. While I was busy rehearsing what I was going to say, I fell asleep. When we arrived home, all I could think about was finding some fluid, non-alcoholic. My mouth tasted like one of the spit-and-sawdust floors that were becoming so popular in Edinburgh's trendy Leith wine bars.

'Evening, officer,' my father said. I stumbled past him and made my way to the kitchen for a drink of water. 'I'm so sorry,' I heard him say.

'We think she might need some help,' the policewoman was saying, in a quasi-caring tone.

My hand closed around the glass. I raised it high above my head. I was thinking about flinging it – at something, someone. I knew I was still a bit pissed, still able to disguise the fear I really felt.

My father was worming his way out of everything as only he could. 'I'm sorry. It won't happen again,' he said, so meekly, shorthand for: 'Let's just carry on as if nothing has happened. Don't let's open this particular can of worms.'

I knew his pattern off by heart, could read between all his well-rehearsed lines. I wanted to break the glass, pick up one of the shattered pieces and drag its jagged edge across his face. Instead I aimed the glass at the window, prepared to throw it. I wanted to see it splinter into lots of little pieces but changed my mind. Things were bad enough. An act of protest from me wasn't going to help.

I heard the front door close and my father clear his throat as he approached the kitchen. He came in, filled the kettle and pulled down the switch, watching me stand with the glass still raised above my head, a gesture he chose to ignore.

'I'll make us some tea,' he said, his tone almost nonchalant. 'You know we'll stand by you when this goes to court.'

He never mentioned it again.

Every so often he'd say: 'You're just like your mother, Nicola,' as if this was the worst possible destiny I could have chosen. I don't think he ever forgave me for being in his car when I was stopped by the police. He didn't mind so much when I was stopped again in St Andrews, well over the limit, a week later. I was in my own car that time and away from home so his cronies at work were less likely to find out. A story about me appeared in one of the local papers. I dreaded him finding that out. St Andrews didn't know about Edinburgh and vice versa, so I kept very quiet. I got a lawyer to deal with both court cases and ended up paying two hefty fines.

My nights were often disturbed after visits home. I'd be asleep, dreaming that I'm standing outside my flat, at one end of a narrow lane, watching something resembling a vegetable approach from the opposite end. It's huge and green with white stalks. It's a cauliflower, a cabbage, something like that. I can't quite make it out. It's holding up a mirror, inviting me to look at my reflection. I try to look but can't take my eyes off the vegetable. It's getting bigger and bigger, spreading over the road ahead. I look to the right and left of it, but there's no way past it, no escape. It's rubbing up against me now.

I catch a scent clinging to its leaves, familiar, a big cauliflower reeking of something sickly: vodka on someone else's breath. They think it doesn't smell but I can always smell it.

I hold up my arms to protect myself, try to back away. There's nowhere to go, just a hard surface against which I push and push. Nothing gives.

No air in my lungs. I want air. All I can hear is a pounding sound, my heart in my ears in the darkness, a mass of suspense. Where's the light, where is the light? Where am I? Dying in some alien place? I want to die somewhere familiar. Not here, not now, not like this.

Stuck somewhere between waking and sleeping, I struggle to breathe. There is confusion, sweat, the rapid beat of my heart, darkness and this heavy, heavy load. I must get up, out of here, if I am to live. I try again to suck in air, but there is none and I don't have long to go.

I'm awake. I'm not dead.

I leap up, still clutching my aching chest. If I don't

breathe soon I'll burst, with palpitations, with this sweat and dizziness. I'm aware of this feeling of doom, of danger, gesturing, beckoning. It came on so suddenly and I still can't catch my breath.

I'm dying. Yes, I am dying after all. I have to get out of this place. I am on my feet, bare feet on a soft surface, like a carpet but not a carpet. It feels like a good place to die. I try to inhale, to catch my breath, but nothing, just vanishing reality. I'm going, leaving early, without saying goodbye.

Someone says something, faceless, soundless. The words are in my head. I'm about to respond when I realise there's no one there. I start groping, don't know where I am, don't care; only care that I can't breathe.

There is a wall. I stretch out my arms and lean into what feels like wallpaper. I feel something soft and velvety in my right hand. I clutch at it, pull, until folds of the soft material pour into my damp hand. Then I grab at it with both hands, pulling and tearing it away from the wall. There's a ripping sound, something long and narrow, the curtain rail crashes to the floor, just missing my head by a fraction of an inch. It hits my shoulder and I jump away, banging my leg on whatever I'd been lying on.

Instantly, I know where I am: back in my bedroom at home, dying.

There's one last hope: get to the front door, run

outside, find someone who can save me, help me to breathe again. I crouch down, struggle with the darkness, refusing to give in to my body's desire to pass out, put an end to the fight.

Let go of the curtains, avoid falling over the rail now lying on the floor, edge around the darkened room towards the open doorway out into the hall and over to the front door. Within seconds, I'm running down the street, screaming, running like the wind when my shoe catches on an invisible wire and something clicks inside my head. I see familiar objects in the half-light: a street lamp casting orange shadows, a row of shops. Hey, I know this street. It's in Bruntsfield. It runs past my house, with the friendly launderette, the small coffee shop and the lumps of chewing-gum on the pavement.

I look at my reflection in a shop window – see a lunatic in a long black T-shirt, a dark shape with flailing arms and flyaway legs, a suitable case for asylum. A ghost or silhouette?

Please don't let anyone ask me what happened, I can't explain.

Then I try again, a deep, deep inhalation which, this time, does catch air. Sweet breath bolts down my throat, filling my chest and lungs. I hold it down, relish the beauty of the moment, quiver with life and the realisation I am not going to die. Not this time.

I stand, reflect on my narrow escape, make an effort to

breathe in and out, sucking and blowing, looking for the black spectre in the shop window. She has gone – the lunatic. Left behind is my reflection. A man scurries past on the other side of the road, trying not to look, squinting nevertheless at the sight of a young woman in the street in the middle of the night.

Fear has a hierarchy. Normally I might have feared this stranger seeing me here in my nightie. Instead I feel like waving. I have just dug myself out of the quicksand and cannot feel fear at the sight of a mere man in the street. I go back home, lie down on my bed and vow to put the curtain rail back in the morning.

# Chapter 11

# Naked but Not Ashamed

I frittered away my time at St Andrews University on a sea of alcohol, blitzed from Raisin Monday, a tradition where new students are assisted by their seniors in adapting to university life, through to my fourth year when I abandoned an honours degree for an ordinary. I developed an air of false confidence, fuelled by drink, but behaved as if possessed by a delinquent. I disrupted classes, infuriated my lecturers. While successful in philosophy, I consistently made a fool of myself in my daily life as a student. I was miserable, would have given anything to go back into hospital and stay there, even though my hips were relatively cured by that time. People don't usually want to be disabled, but, at that stage in my life, I did, with all my heart.

In 1970, I met a gentle marine biologist called Colin at the university. I was twenty and he was my first and last-but-one serious boyfriend. I had plenty of offers over the years, of sex not friendship. I refused to allow men to know me, always made sure there was a protective layer of alcohol between myself and them. I did have a few people who remained consistent, no matter what I did, right through university, one a perceptive man called Ron Glasgow who, with his friends Peter and Margaret West, spent a lot of time sticking close when most other people had written me off as damaged goods.

On my twenty-first birthday, a GP had me admitted to a prison masquerading as a psychiatric hospital in Fife where a thoroughly unpleasant doctor treated me for schizophrenia, filling me with weird pills and injections. Colin was confused. He came to see me a couple of times but didn't really know what to do for the best. I managed to escape from the ward one evening as the day staff handed over to the night nurses. I knew my car was somewhere in the hospital grounds, tracked it down and drove to Edinburgh, despite being so drugged I was virtually unable to see straight. I had no idea what drugs I'd been given but they were strong.

Once home, I behaved oddly, heard voices, imagined I was being followed around. I now know that you can suffer from temporary schizophrenia. Had there been some support available at home, I might have recovered without having to be hospitalised, but my parents promptly had me admitted to the Royal Edinburgh

Hospital for three months of group therapy. The theory was that when patients join a group, they interact freely with others and recreate the problems that brought them into therapy in the first place. I fitted in well, excelled at bringing other people out of themselves, so the doctor in charge told me, but didn't make much progress personally. If I learned anything from the experience, it was that my parents were the cause of my mental state, far more than any schizophrenia. My mother's drinking and my father's coldness and bad temper proved a deadly combination. I thrived in hospital, away from them, but the minute I went home, the stress and fear took over again.

In those days, psychiatric hospitals catered for people's mental states – but woe betide anyone who had anything physically wrong with them. I lost a lot of weight during those two months and my legs ached constantly. The nurses wouldn't give me any painkillers, saying I had to work through the reasons for the pain, that they were psychological. A friend brought me in some painkillers, about ten, in a large bottle where previously there had been a hundred. One of the nurses found the bottle by my bed. She insisted I was slurring my words – I wasn't – and immediately assumed I had taken an overdose. No matter how hard I tried to convince her I hadn't, she refused to believe me and had me transferred to the Poisons Unit at Edinburgh Royal Infirmary, where I lay strapped to a bed, unable to move. I was there for a stomach pump, one of the most frightening experiences of my life, probably because I was wide-awake at the time. My parents were nowhere to be seen.

They inserted a tube up my nose, down into my stomach, then made me gag for what felt like several hours. They did this by passing cold water into my stomach and then out again through a tube into a bucket. The staff kept saying they couldn't find anything; trying again, hoping they would eventually find my so-called overdose. It was like being strangled very slowly. Afterwards, I was kept in hospital overnight and forced to discuss my suicide attempt with yet another psychiatrist. It put me off the profession for life. When he heard what I had supposedly done, my father said he wasn't surprised. My mother was shocked but believed me after my friend had convinced her it wasn't a suicide attempt, that she had brought in an almost empty bottle.

I felt at this stage that my parents wanted to wash their hands of me. I was no longer of any use to them and had become more trouble than I was worth. Neither my mother nor my father actually wanted to parent. My father's nit-picking was constant; his put-downs and his temper sapped any energy I possessed. To the outside world, he presented himself as a good, caring doctor, but the minute he got home, he changed personality. People said he was shy, which he was, but not with me. My mother called him a street saint and house bugger, which perfectly described his behaviour. She was no better, however, depending on her children to look after her instead of the other way around. Like my father, she also appeared, on the surface, to cope well, yet could barely function when left to be a mother and homemaker.

It was almost impossible to believe how privileged my mother's own childhood had been; her family's beautiful homes in Guernsey and London, the servants, a first-class education at a top girls' school, Roedean, in England. She had swallowed the silver spoon she'd been born with and had nothing left over. She hardly ever saw her father. Her mother, Edith, became obsessed with the idea that her oldest daughter, with her good looks and brains, would end up too full of herself, so she kept telling my mother she was ugly. This brutal, rudimentary psychology caused my mother to grow up with no confidence at all; a multi-faceted failing she managed to pass onto me.

How she fell so dramatically from all this grace was a question I repeatedly asked myself. The right man might have carried her through the worst of her insecurities, brought out her talents as a doctor and a mother; but the wrong one, my father, sat on her as hard as he could and squashed every last ounce of potential out of her.

By the early seventies, my mother was in a pitiful state. Since I had come back from teaching in France to live in

Scotland and go to university, she cottoned on to the fact that I was once again there for her. She started phoning me, drunk yet just as anxious, at 8 a.m. each day. This went on all through my university life. The calming effect of drink had lessened and she always needed more. Michael said he had been at the house one time and taken delivery of a dozen bottles of cooking sherry. She was drinking more than ever. I'd talk to her on the phone then replace the receiver, pick up a large cushion I kept close to the phone and bash it repeatedly against the wall; harder and harder until, one day, I injured my arm and had to stop doing it. But I was so frustrated.

One day, she brought up the subject of Colin.

'You've been together a while now,' she said, as if a certain duration gave her the right to intervene. 'You must bring him home, Nic, I'm dying to meet him. Why are you being so secretive?'

'You know why,' I responded, unable to keep that ever-present note of cruelty out of my voice.

'Darling, I won't drink, I promise,' Mummy said, 'not in front of your boyfriend. Bring him for a meal and everything will be fine.'

We'd discussed it many times, conversations which invariably concluded with her in her room, drunk, and me in the living room, irate. Colin was my first chance at happiness, I kept keep telling her, why did she want to spoil it? Then she'd wheedle and plead and sulk until, eventually, one day, I caved in and agreed to ask Colin round for dinner. I'd have to let them meet at some point, I reasoned. Together we planned a menu: pasta and a special sauce she'd learned to make on an Italian cookery course.

'Remember how you made me do that evening class in Italian cooking?' she continued to chat, now she had got her own way. "Do an evening class in cooking, Mummy, for God's sake," you said. "Apart from improving your lousy cooking, you might meet a nice bloke." How charming. Remember all the men I met in that cookery class? Every single one I fancied was queer. The only thing they wanted to whip up was each other.'

I smiled.

'Anyway, then we'll have fresh strawberries and cream, the berries soaked overnight in a lemon marinade,' she decided.

Mummy bought a new outfit that she kept trying on, as if for a wedding, wandering about the house, seeking my approval, having more fun than she'd had for a long time. I actually began to dare to look forward to the evening. She wanted one of two things: either that I would do the right thing and get married or that Colin would like her and we'd both be round at the house more often. I'd partially prepared Colin for meeting my mother, keeping back the bits I didn't think he needed to know. He knew my mother drank, but not to such an extent. He knew my father had a stinking temper, but not that he was a tormented man who couldn't cope with his lot in life.

There were still anxieties at the back of my mind about the visit. Would she really be abstemious for once or would she let me down, as usual? In the end, I was so worried I decided to stay at home the night before to help her with preparations. We had a great evening, chatting, digging out some good silver from a box in the loft and a white tablecloth, mostly unused, even examining family photographs.

Since the build-up had been such plain sailing, I could scarcely believe it when I heard her on the phone the following morning at 7 a.m.

'Hello, is that Harvey's?' She was phoning the grocer's from whom she got most of her alcohol. I could hear her voice clear as a bell from my bedroom, even though she was speaking quietly.

'I know I'm a bit early, but there are a few things we need,' I heard her say, in a hoarse voice, as if she was trying to keep it low. 'I'd like some soap powder, the usual brand, a jar of coffee, a packet of digestive biscuits, oh, and a bottle of red wine, no, make that two. And one of vodka. We've got guests.'

As I lay in bed, silently fuming, the conversation made my heart stand still. That was always her pattern: make up a few respectable items of shopping then drop in the bottles. It was so obvious. If I'd had a gun that morning, I swear I'd have gone out onto the landing and put a bullet straight through her heart, what was left of it. The woman needed a drink to face her own shadow. I didn't feel sorry for her any more although, in retrospect, I suppose I should have done. I was judgemental of my mother's drinking in a way I never was of my own. By this stage, I was fed up with the whole family in relation to my mother; how I wished my father or brothers would do more to help her.

When the bell rang at 8 a.m., the front door opened abruptly. She must have been waiting right there in front of it, preparing panther-like to pounce, desperate to get her hands on the booze. I sat up in bed.

'I'm sorry to ask,' I heard her say in her best wheedling tone, 'but I need the wine for cooking this morning and can't find the corkscrew anywhere. Could you possibly open one of the bottles for me?'

As the suction sound of the cork popping echoed up the stairs, I cringed.

'Thank you, thank you so much,' she said and closed the door, desperate to get back inside and be alone with her prize. She was going to start with the wine and leave the strong stuff until last.

I got out of bed and put on my dressing gown. By the time I reached the stairs, my fury was ready to erupt. She was coming up the stairs to hide the bottles in her bedroom, leaving a small bag of shopping at the bottom of the stairs.

'You promised you wouldn't,' I spat out the words in a terrible voice I didn't recognise. 'Just this once, you promised. "Oh, bring Colin home, please, darling,"' I mimicked. '"You must let me meet him. Of course I won't drink, not on such an important occasion." And here he is, coming today, and you've got booze being delivered – opened, even – at the crack of dawn.'

My mother had stopped halfway up the stairs and was looking down, as if inspecting the worn carpet, sliding her left hand up and down the banister in what, on the face of it, seemed like panic.

'Nic, forgive me,' she started. 'I just can't face . . .'

'Shut the fuck up!' I shouted, glowering down at her from the vantage point of the top step. 'You're always bloody sorry. You don't care about me or anything else. You, you . . .' I was stammering I was so angry.

'Shut your bloody mouth, you spoiled bitch.'

My mother had spoken. The change in her mood quite dramatic; the words out before she could stop herself. She seemed shocked by their impact, embarrassed by their sheer defiance, yet oddly reassured, as if she had suddenly realised she still had a right to get angry.

'It's easy for you, isn't it?'

My mother's cheeks burned bright red as she clutched the banister again, knuckles straining to hang on.

'You've got a cushy life, popping in here every time you want something from me, pretending to your father you look after me, when you never so much as lift a finger to help. All you ever do is spy, see how much I've been drinking and report back to him. If you're not sniffing my breath, you're snooping in the laundry basket and my drawers, looking for empties. Don't think I don't know.

' "Did you drink this?" and "Did you drink that?" You're even worse than him and, believe me, being worse than that bastard takes some doing.' She was trembling from head to toe, yet warming to her theme.

'You know what it's like to suffer, don't you, Nicola? You understand what it's like not to be able to face the next day, to feel so screwed up that only a drink can put you at some kind of peace with yourself? I know you do. I've seen you. How come it's okay for you but not for me? I know what you're after: my money. You'd be better off in every way if I were dead. Then you can have your precious Colin and no nuisance mother to spoil everything for you.'

Her speech didn't succeed in garnering any pity. She was always bringing up the subject of her money. I don't think she really believed we were waiting for her to die so we could have it. She used it to shut us up when we were angry with her about her drinking.

I was furious, the angriest I'd ever been. I came down the stairs to her level.

'How would you know anything about my suffering?' I screamed back. 'You haven't a clue, have you? You're always out of your face, that's why. You're never here, not really here, not like a proper mother would be. You've never been here for any of us.'

I knew that would hurt, that I'd have the satisfaction of seeing real pain make a brief appearance on her face.

'You don't know the meaning of the word "mother". Don't kid me that you've suffered. How, pray? You've never had to go without in your whole life, never had to wonder where your next meal was coming from, let alone your next drink. You've had it all on a plate with a family to clear up after you as well.' I was beside myself. I was shouting. As a child I had never really been aware of all the rage I contained. Now it spilled out everywhere.

'You should go see what it's like to lose everything through drink – your home, your children, your health and friends.' I knew it sounded pious but I'd been working as a volunteer at a centre for down-and-outs in Edinburgh's Grassmarket, with men and women who slept all night on sheets of newspaper. If they wet the floor they were banned from the hostel.

'You've already lost most of your friends, though, haven't you?' I was still shouting at her. 'Maybe if you lost everything else, you might sit up and take notice. As long as I'm here to pick up the pieces, it's too easy for you to carry on, isn't it?'

My words were so loud they echoed, rushed up and down the stairs before crash landing in our ears; all my loathing of her, my crushing disappointment, all the lies I'd tolerated for so long. At that moment my mother was vermin, the lowest of life forms, and this was a conversation I should have had with her years ago.

'You and Daddy, you're as bad as each other,' I went on. 'He offers me money to look after you when you're pissed, just so he can go and climb his mountains.'

She winced at this information, as if she hadn't been familiar with her husband's unorthodox methods of childrearing.

'As far as you're concerned, it's "Just knock it back and Nicola will get me off the floor; a few more bottles of vodka and Nicola can turn off the fire and the cooker; Nicola will help me out of the bath and clean up the sick." Drink yourself to death and Nicola will arrange the funeral.

'Well, just you wait, because one of these days, when you're lying face down in your own vomit . . . there won't be anyone left to clean up your mess.'

At that point her knees buckled and she collapsed on the stairs. I had been cruel. And I had almost enjoyed every moment of it. She was crying, her face shiny with fresh tears. She began to act as if she'd lost it altogether: screaming and yelling, bashing her head against the banister until streaks of blood appeared in her hair; her overreaction intended to stop me shouting. I ran back upstairs and phoned her GP, told the receptionist my mother was having some kind of breakdown, that I was on my own and someone had to come immediately. On the rare occasions I did ask for the GP's help, I always said I was on my own. In that respect they were like the Automobile Association and came more quickly, even if they did only do a temporary patch-up.

It wasn't until later I realised she had held onto her bottles in the frenzy, managed to spirit them off to her room to hide before the doctor arrived. I already had this particular GP down as an ill-informed cretin. He gave her a couple of strong tranquillisers, said she'd be fine by the evening, too stupid or naïve to realise that she loved tranquillisers, liked nothing better than pills, pills and more pills washed down with a pint of cooking sherry or cheap wine.

That night Colin came round as planned. I told him what had happened, and we decided to carry on as normal. I had cooked a meal, so the two of us sat in the dining room and ate on our own. Mummy hadn't surfaced since the GP left, knocked out by the tranquillisers and, no doubt, all the vodka and wine. The house was eerily quiet. For me there was something reassuring about being on home ground with Colin, no matter how bad the circumstances. I felt confident for once. Safe, yet strangely aware that this was the last place I could feel safe with any certainty. I showed him round the house. He observed that a lot of the doors were closed and I explained that my father didn't really like people in the house, not realising at the time how odd it must have sounded. I served the meal, we ate and he seemed to savour every mouthful. We had a great time.

Towards the end of the evening, we were deep in conversation when the door handle began to move from side to side, the way it always did when Mummy was too drunk to open a door normally. It was a sign, a warning. You'd be sitting quietly, minding your own business, and the handle would start to make a noise, a sort of furtive, fumbling sound. When I was little, Peter and I would count how many times she turned the handle before managing to open the door. Once we counted thirty-eight. We were laughing so much we didn't see her throw up all over the floor before turning round to go back to bed again; although cleaning up the sick while Pete went to watch telly had made me cry and cry.

Colin and I stopped talking, mesmerised by the door handle's perpetual motion. I wanted to explain, say something, but I'd left it too late. As the door finally opened, I could see him take a deep breath, preparing to greet a possible mother-in-law. That was when Mummy chose to stumble into the room, totally naked, head bent forward, intent on finding something to eat in the kitchen. Colin didn't move, hardly looked up from the position in which he was frozen.

My mother's face was streaked with make-up, her mottled thighs covered in black bruises from bumping into furniture. Her backside wobbled along behind her, entering the room a few seconds after she did. Bleary-eyed, she turned to look at the clock ticking away on the mantelpiece and squinted, unable to make out the time. She swayed, then lurched against the dresser, setting the wine glasses and crystal flagons rattling in their cupboards. Straightening up, she squinted at us sitting at the table, barely registering the agony on my face, ignoring Colin, who was still frozen to his seat, hardly daring to breathe. Every inch of the room screamed out in shame and panic. Gradually it dawned on my mother that something was wrong, although she wasn't quite sure what. The strange man sitting with her daughter had something to do with it, that much was clear.

'Hi,' she said, her voice thick with alcohol, 'I'm Nicola's mother. How are you?'

Colin struggled to smile, held out his hand but, as she turned and wobbled back out of the room, Colin leaned forward, head in his hands, and let out a long groan.

I broke down and wept, shaking and sobbing. 'I'm so sorry,' I repeated, 'I should have known better than to ask you here.'

Colin got up to make us some coffee, asking where the

cups were, busying himself with finding the kettle. In total silence, he made two cups, sat down and looked at me. He proceeded to tell me that, up until then, he had dismissed most of what I'd said about my mother as exaggeration. Now, he felt he understood me better. It was a kind remark, yet I was convinced what he had seen would put him right off.

As midnight approached, we heard the sound of sobbing from Mummy's bedroom. It was dreadful, lonely, filling the whole house; so distressing I felt I had to ask Colin to leave. Before going slowly downstairs, he put his arms round me and held me, thanking me for a great evening. I almost believed he had enjoyed it. An hour later, drink got the better of Mummy's misery and she fell silent, ready to sleep off yet another family trauma caused, as usual, by her.

I drank more during the time I was with Colin than ever, more than I had in France, yet we stayed together, on and off, for five years. At times I felt I was turning out to be the one thing I dreaded: my mother. Like her, whenever I was called upon to make an impression, to be confident, I needed drink to make it happen.

After meeting my mother, Colin suspected I'd been badly affected by her drinking and, throughout our relationship, he suffered agonies of embarrassment as a result of going out with me. One evening, just before he was due to pick me up at the cottage where I lived near St Andrew's, I was enjoying a warm, soapy bath, sipping a glass of Chianti, my head resting against a rubber pillow stuck to the enamel. On the wall was a Botticelli print, lit from above by a narrow strip-light inside a metal fixture. I liked having it in the bathroom, even though steam from the bath was already dissolving the frame. Two burning candles made the bathroom smell of jasmine. I remember looking at the wine bottle sitting on a tiled shelf behind the bath and sighing. It was half empty. But drinking it out of a glass in the bath made me feel sort of normal, almost civilised, states I had convinced myself were out of my reach.

Colin was due in an hour. My farm cottage was about half an hour away from where he lived with some of his diving mates. Unlike me, Colin was always on time. I still had to dress and put on some make-up. I stayed in the warm water for another ten minutes, blew out the candles and hauled myself out of the bath as the water drained away. Catching sight of my stomach in the mirror, I inhaled deeply, holding it in as I towelled myself dry. I had a good figure, well proportioned with most of the flesh in the right places, except for this grotesque midriff, a relatively new development, which, a few years later, would nearly kill me. I didn't realise at that point it was a sign of alcohol poisoning.

It wasn't even a belly, more of a swelling right in the

middle of my stomach, around the abdomen. Sometimes it felt sensitive to touch, raw. There was nausea as well as violent pain, especially when I'd had a drink, but I didn't want to think about that. On my last visit home, I had almost asked Mummy what might have caused it, thinking she'd remember from her medical studies, but thought better of it – just in case it did have something to do with drink.

I brushed my hair, encouraging it to curl out at the shoulders before pinning it back to apply my make-up. I sat down at my dressing table, pulled my make-up bag out of one of the drawers and slapped on some tan foundation, not too orange, more golden brown, added a little eye shadow, navy mascara and lots of the red lipstick Colin liked, before pulling on a red dress and high heels.

When I heard the doorbell, I grabbed the bottle and downed the rest of the contents before stuffing it into a wastepaper basket and opening the front door. He didn't want to come in, said we were running late. Feeling pissed, I turned off all the lights apart from the one in the hall, pocketed my keys and went to join him. We were going out to a restaurant for dinner with some of his friends.

Colin drove fast through back streets I didn't know, finally searching for a parking place in Market Street where he locked the car and we headed for the restaurant.

'It's Italian,' Colin said. 'Cosy, friendly, clean, excellent food.'

As he held the door open for me, he waved to a party of four seated right in the centre of the restaurant, two other couples in their early twenties. A waiter, who followed us to the table, took my coat, stroking my arms gently as he removed it. The action was scarcely perceptible but people will do anything they like to drunk women. He was giving me the eye, even though he knew I was with a boyfriend. I guessed he was doing it because I was drunk, yet I somehow convinced myself he found me attractive.

My heart was racing. I couldn't believe I still felt nervous after a whole bottle of wine. Usually, one bottle did the trick. I hoped Colin's friends weren't marine biologists but decided, when I sat down, that they were; something to do with the jokes they told and the earnest way they looked at me.

His four pals, it turned out, were PhD students. My worst nightmare.

'This is Nicola,' Colin said, putting an arm around my shoulders and sitting down beside me. He introduced Jeremy, Jane, Terry and Laura. I smiled at them, clutching Colin's hand under the table. I was afraid they wouldn't like me, be too sophisticated, talk about subjects of which I knew nothing. Paranoia lingered at the table. I needed a drink. Jeremy must have read my mind.

'Gin, vodka, wine, champagne, what's your tipple, Nicola?'

'I'll have a vodka and tonic,' I said, sounding merry already, smiling at Jeremy. I was beginning to feel sleepy. Long soak in the hot bath, bottle of wine, mellow. I remembered Colin's accusation the last time we went out – that I'd knocked back spirits like water.

'I'll drink this one slowly,' I told myself grimly, watching his face for any hint of disapproval. There was none.

'So, do tell, how's university treating you?' Terry asked. He gestured towards Colin. 'Is he hindering your studies?'

'Not a bit of it,' I said and turned to stroke Colin's hair, surprised at how thick and smooth it felt. Usually, his hair was unruly. He was forever running his fingers through it in exasperation, which should have made it greasy, but it flopped and bounced all over the place. He grinned at me.

I downed my drink. Hey, why was I going so fast? I'd already had my warm-up and normally stuck to my regular going-out routine: a bottle of wine to kick off so I wouldn't feel nervous, a few slow drinks during the evening then as much as I wanted to knock me out at bedtime. Sometimes, Colin and I stayed together and he drank a fair amount as well, but that was normal among students. They knew when to stop and they didn't sit in public toilets having a slug because they were afraid they couldn't cope. I hated feeling out of my league, which I did most of the time. Fortunately, before I could ask for another drink, which would have upset Colin, a waiter put two bottles of wine on the table and Jeremy immediately poured me a large glass. As I sipped, I realised I wanted to go to the loo, wine running straight through me.

'Excuse me,' I muttered, tried to stand up but sat straight back down again.

'Oh dear, someone's been on the piss already this evening.' It was Jeremy.

'I have not,' I shouted, but my objection felt as feeble as my legs. This time I managed to stand up, very slowly and deliberately. I had already clocked the loo, over in a far corner, next to the entrance. My new friends were staring at me as I swayed off, fascinated either by my bum or my skill at staying upright. I was used to this situation, like a naval officer with years of experience who's familiar with every pitch and roll. Mind you, the sea was a bit rough tonight. I vaguely took in Colin's pinched face. Even though I rarely experienced shame myself, I recognised it immediately in somebody else.

The waiter who had taken my coat was watching me from beneath hooded, sexy eyes. I winked at him and he smiled back, too readily, a shark on the prowl. He jumped to hold open the toilet door as I prepared to sail through it, unaware that he was right behind me. In the small, dark corridor that ran past the Ladies and smelled of spices, garlic and bleach, the waiter drew me towards him. He felt sensuous, hairy and strong. He was kissing me, ramming his salami-flavoured tongue down my throat until I could scarcely breathe. I didn't object, though. It was too exciting to ask him to stop and I was too pissed anyway.

He pushed open the door of the Ladies and bundled me inside, snibbing the lock behind us. One enormous hand slithered up my dress, inside my pants and yanked them down far enough for him to penetrate me. Even in my haze, I knew he couldn't believe his luck. We were off. He moaned, muttering 'Bella, bella' every few seconds, banging my head against the toilet wall, passion or oblivion, I wasn't sure which. Then, he zipped up his trousers, kissed my cheek and was gone, as if he'd just been handing me the bill.

It was something I did when drunk, went along with a person's wishes because I couldn't be bothered fighting. When you're overwhelmed by your own sense of worthlessness, nothing matters, not even someone treating you as badly as this.

Christ, I wished I'd had another one of those miniatures in my bag. Still, Jeremy would pour me more wine, no matter what Colin said.

When I walked back into the restaurant, the oily

waiter was at our table, holding back my seat so I could sit down. Our eyes met: 'Three-minute fuckwit,' I muttered in his ear. His expressionless smile didn't alter one iota. He just slithered away.

Colin was staring oddly, his eyebrows raised as he put his arm round me to ask if I was okay.

'You were away so long,' he said. 'I missed you.'

I smiled, picked up my glass to gulp down some more wine but the glass wavered then stopped dead in mid-air. The suddenness with which Colin tried to wrench it from my hand shocked me. His pals, who had been discussing management problems in their department, stopped talking as an uneasy silence descended. I was too drunk to argue with Colin, so sat sulking, both elbows on the table, glugging my red wine every time he looked the other way. I could feel my right elbow slipping to one side and my eyes desperately trying to close. Every time I dragged my arm back, it slipped away again.

My starter, a mix of prawns, avocado and some brown lettuce, sat in front of me, untouched. I stared at the pink sauce and my mouth started watering, filling up with saliva. Then it happened and the memory will stay with me for the rest of my life. I was violently sick all over my beautiful prawns.

# Chapter 12

# Death's Door

Not surprisingly, the prawn incident proved the one that broke the camel's back. Colin and I finished. Despite being drunk most of the time I managed to graduate with a degree in Moral Philosophy and English. But I didn't have a clue what I wanted to do next. My mother wanted me to go back to living at home, to work in Edinburgh. But I decided to take a break from Scotland and travel. I had a friend who was making a fortune teaching English in Japan so I applied to work for several large companies with employees who needed to learn English, and was taken on. I packed up my home, flung a few possessions in a bag, and left Edinburgh for a suburb of Nagoya, Southern Japan, called Ikeshita. It was a pokey place, with streets that smelled of garlic, herbs and petrol. The nightlife was perpetual. Most of the people I met slept all day and partied all night. I put my classes off until the afternoon and joined in. It wasn't long before I was drinking in the mornings as well.

In the seventies, I loved sub-aqua diving, a sport I had learned from Colin. I'd done all the training and passed the test for sinking diving equipment to the bottom of a swimming pool and retrieving it piece by piece. It wasn't the sort of sport you could mix with a drinking lifestyle. I was asking for something bad to happen and it did, rather ironically on the one day I didn't have a drink before breakfast. It was June in Japan, the height of the cherry-blossom season, and I'd had at least a litre of sake, rice wine, the night before. Drinking it was similar, I imagine, to sucking sardines, but I did it anyway. That night I drank so much I remember starting to walk backwards while attempting to go uphill on my way home. It made my friends laugh. The morning after, I had the shakes and a bout of paranoia but I wasn't drunk.

I was a good swimmer but never really gave much thought to my old diving training. When you drink for a living, you take risks. You don't have to be drunk to sample danger, yet everything points you in its direction. It's part and parcel of the liquid lifestyle. That was how I came to do a sub-aqua roll dive, off the side of a pool, in deepest, darkest Japan one morning in 1976, sober, stone cold. Hands by my side, head bowed forward, in I went: a quick roll and then clunk, my head struck the concrete bottom of the pool.

From the edge of the pool, the water looked so deep. I discovered later, too late, that the water was dirty. The signs warning you not to dive are all in Japanese Kanji, which I hadn't bothered to learn. 'More wine, please,' and 'Another gin and tonic' were my phrasebook mantras.

There was something like a thunderstorm inside my head as my skull smashed against the bottom of the pool. No pain, just blood, already turning the murky water orange. My mouth slowly filled up with chlorinated water; no air, no power in my arms or legs, no way of struggling back to the surface. I was swallowing water, desperate for air, dicing with death, here in this pool surrounded by strange signs.

Out of nowhere, from some dark recess of my brain, came the magic word: 'Float.' Louder and louder: 'Float, float, float.' With all the will I could muster, I forced my body to relax. I floated to the surface, choked, spluttered, gasped for delicious air. This time I held my breath before sinking back down into the cloudy pool again. I remembered to breathe out through my nose then float up again for air. I was not, repeat not, going to die.

One minute I'd been beside the pool, fairly fit and able, pushing my body to perform a trick of the diving trade; the next I was a whimpering, cowering thing, unable to stand up; a puppet but with no one to pull the strings.

After a while, it felt like hours but was probably

minutes, two lifeguards came running along the poolside; Japanese guys, small and sturdy. They jumped into the water and made their first big mistake, tried to drag me up the pool steps. I couldn't coordinate myself or stand up. Nor could I speak enough Japanese to suggest they didn't move me. As I lay beside the pool, one of them went away to use the phone.

'We take you to hospital for X-ray,' he said when he returned.

After half an hour of lying cold and prone at the poolside, I was bundled into a small ambulance and we screeched through the busy streets of Nagoya, siren blaring. I didn't have a clue what was wrong. The staff took X-rays and charged me a lot of money for them then sent me to another, larger hospital. Here, a tubby man in a white coat decided to tell me what was wrong.

'You have broken your neck,' he announced grandly. 'If you move, you may die. You will be in hospital for a long, long time. Our hospital.' He turned to examine the X-rays then said, with devastating frankness, 'We think you may end up a vegetable.'

I laughed. What else could I do? I could feel nothing down my left side and assumed I was paralysed. The doctor seemed to agree, said I was very close to decomposition: 'Your neck is still attached – only just – by a quarter of an inch. You're lucky to be alive.'

I wasn't so sure. I didn't feel particularly lucky. The

Japanese medics always said what they [...]
but never explained why. When the tubby [...]
'Once Nurse Kaoru has shaved your head, I am g[...]
nail in fifteen kilograms of traction,' I made a noise li[...]
a cat being run over. Was he going to hammer nails into
the sides of my head? And what about my hair? I couldn't
bear to be bald. The nurse brought me a mirror, which
revealed my hair was all matted with blood, most of it
dried and shrivelled. She shaved off my hair then
immediately removed the mirror, sparing me any further
distress. The doctor screwed what did appear to be nails
into my head. It didn't hurt, but it did feel distinctly
weird, especially when he hung fifteen kilograms behind
my bed, a dead weight that created strange sensations
and upset my sense of balance. My head would spin, I'd
grab the sides of the bed and begin to feel as if I was
turning upside down, as if I was suspended from the
ceiling, screaming for help. This frequent occurrence
wasn't helped by Japanese people who brought flowers
when they visited and hung them upside down,
according to their custom.

On the first day, three men came into my room,
bowing and scraping and muttering in Japanese, carrying
boxes, gifts. They couldn't speak any English, unusual in
Japan. A nurse told me they said they'd come back. I
discovered they were the owners of the pool in which I'd
had the accident. They made many visits, no doubt

...able to move or see ...te ceiling. If I strained ...ut the tree outside my ... by its leaves the changing ...y one loyal companion was ...n made its way painstakingly ... the other side of the room and back a... ..., month after month.

The ques... ...never ending. Was I going to die? I didn't know. Was I going to be paralysed for good? No one would say. How would I adjust? Would my family care? They didn't phone, they didn't write. A friend eventually wrote and told me my mother was drinking heavily, said she'd seen her stumbling in the street. My accident had provided her with the perfect excuse to drink even more.

My father had gone to work in Sweden for a few months and was planning to find work for six months of the year over there from now on. Peter and his wife, Lindsay, had returned from Australia and were spending more time with Mummy. They even lived at home for a while. My mother adored Lindsay, turned to her for affection when she failed to get it from her own children. During the years my mother lay dying, only Lindsay realised that she was never going to tackle her addiction, that there was nothing anyone could do. My sister-in-law gave her the compassion she craved.

In my darker moments, I wondered about all the years I had spent in a wheelchair. Why me again? What on earth had I done? I didn't know anybody who'd had so many operations. Sometimes it felt like a punishment. Other times it seemed as if I had found a convenient way out of the human race, hiding away in hospital for the rest of my life, although the thought of never walking again terrified me. I would have to depend on other people and there was nobody there – perhaps anywhere – who was close enough to ask.

The fear rose and fell, came and went, like an unwanted visitor. But at least I hardly ever thought about drink. In hospital, I was perpetually passive. Things were done to me. There was never any need for me to perform or prove myself in any way. I didn't need drink.

On the first day, when the tubby doctor finally went home, I was left with Nurse Kaoru and burst into tears, weeping like a three-year-old, amazed when she joined in and we howled in unison. Struggling with her English, she said: 'Scotland, good, whisky, Nessie, good tea.'

I responded as warmly as the situation allowed, saying if I had been given a choice of where in the world to break my neck, Japan would have been number one on my list. She was over the moon; overjoyed at whatever I had said, even though she wasn't sure what it was. We became firm friends. Whenever I laughed, she bounded off to make me tea as a reward. In hospital, cups of tea are what make the days pass. The first time, she plonked down the tray and said: 'Sorry, no lemon.'

I reassured her: 'That's fine. I'll have milk instead.'

Kaoru would grin, dump the tea down the sink and pour me a glass of milk.

'I'd like the tea too,' I said.

'Two?' she said. 'Nicola San like tea two?'

I ended up with two cups of black tea and one glass of milk, no lemon.

We muddled through. Kaoru found my height presented her with insurmountable problems. My feet hung over the edge of the bed, my nightgown stopped at my navel, and when she discovered the suppositories didn't work because they were too small, she collapsed in hysterics and was unable to work for the rest of the day.

I spent my worst times in that hospital, in isolation, fearing for the future.

Kaoru was the only person to witness 'the miracle'. It took place after I had been in the hospital for six months. We were chatting one afternoon about Scotland, in our limited way, she leaning over my bed, tucking in a blanket, when I screamed out loud. I had felt the weight of her leaning across, meaning the feeling had returned down my left side. She understood straight away.

I had heard so much about the Japanese, about their cruelty during the war, yet could only judge them by my own experience, which was special. I will never forget that day. She bounded out of the room, straight through to the other patients. We were all in our own little side wards; paralysed or partially paralysed. We knew each other by name only, with a bit of medical history thrown in. I could hear Kaoru screaming in the corridor: 'Nicola San. No paralytic.'

Most heartening of all, I could hear the other patients, whom I'd never actually met, whooping for sheer joy. If there was any resentment, no hint of it ever reached me. A university professor next door was totally paralysed after having had exactly the same accident as me. I had met his wife, seen his gorgeous children – and I had seen photos of him. He sent me a note on the day I left the hospital. It said: 'I know how hard it will be for you to go. I wouldn't like to be the one walking away from here, leaving all the others behind. Just remember, don't worry. We are with you, all the way to Scotland.'

I never forgave my parents for not coming out to Japan, for not even phoning, when I broke my neck. I took it as a measure of how much they didn't care. A decade or so later, a friend told me that the most shocking thing she knew about me was that my parents hadn't come out to Japan when I had nearly died. Although I found it devastating, it didn't really surprise me. They had never looked after me when I needed them most. Why should they start now, when I was no longer a child?

My youngest brother, Richard, came to escort me home and his medical training came in useful. I needed three seats of British Airways in order to stretch out and remain stock still the whole way back to Scotland. I wore a sort of straitjacket that gave my spine the support it needed. My head had to be held every time the plane took off and landed.

The journey was terrifying: being winched on and off planes, tolerating a terrible wind in my ears, engines roaring, the perpetual feeling of being thrown around.

Once at the Western General Hospital in Edinburgh they operated, taking a piece of bone out of one of my hips and knitting my spine back together. It took months to heal. I was moved out of hospital and into a nursing home.

When, finally, I went home, I took to drinking huge amounts of alcohol, at least a bottle of vodka a day. I was drinking to get drunk, not just because I was nervous like before. I was heading straight for disaster.

After a year or so in and out of hospital, of partying and generalised mania, a celebration of the fact I was still alive that also felt like a wake, I was mad enough to return to Japan. I hadn't really recovered from the shock of the accident and was less able than ever to cope with the situation at home, so I fled.

Teaching English abroad was a lucrative business,

bringing in enough money to fund my hefty alcohol bill. I would go to the pub after classes, with the students, and stay there until closing time then stagger home alone. Although the students tolerated my behaviour, they must have been secretly appalled. Japanese men – the women didn't drink much back then – tend to get drunk very quickly. The sight, therefore, of a British woman, able to drink a lot more than they could, was particularly repellent.

I was used to wandering home from the pub, through Nagoya's streets, the smell of garlic and herbs mingling with that of cheap scent and cigarette smoke, all wafting on the night air. The city was safe and there were always plenty of other people going home after a night out drinking, dancing, gambling.

The drinker is always the last to see their own deterioration, that slow, steady slide from bad to worse to finished. There were enough warning signs: hot, stabbing pains blasting away at my stomach; a terrible nausea. There were headaches, whole conversations I didn't remember, total blackouts. One problem was that my friends, most of them, accepted me drunk and never really commented on the amount I put away. Some of the local people were embarrassed if I fell over or slurred my words but, being a foreigner, I was already something of a freak in the suburbs, with drink only adding to my oddball status.

I was chewing antacids as if they were breakfast cereal. When I did my weekly shopping I bought fruit, vegetables, bread and antacids, with alcohol next on the list. I had to get the other shopping first in order to slip my bottle underneath it. It was okay to buy drink as part of your shopping but not to buy it on its own. I had learned at least one thing from my mother, after all. One woman I knew in Nagoya attempted to shock me into modifying my behaviour by taking photographs of me lying on my bed, fully clothed, attempting to count a large pile of money I'd earned that week from teaching. When she showed me the pictures a few weeks later, I felt ashamed but also betrayed and hurt. It was an extraordinary thing for a so-called friend to do. Shock tactics have never worked with me. I had been exposed to my mother's drinking for as long as I could remember, and that hadn't been enough to stop me going the same way. She was trying to tell me something but I didn't listen, just avoided her after that.

I knew that drinking in the morning was a sure sign of a problem. There was no way I could pass that off as normal, not even to myself. My routine went like this: arrive at smart Japanese company, ask for the Ladies loo, have a drink from handbag for courage to teach; try desperately hard to conceal the noise of opening can. I always coughed a couple of seconds too late, especially when opening those cans of strong lager. I'd sit there in the loo, imagining I had timed everything perfectly – the tug, the cough, followed by the stinking spray of strong lager. But the tug and spray always came before the cough so other women using the loo would know that, not only was I in there boozing but failing dismally to conceal the fact. I felt incompetent on so many levels. Then I had to discard the empty can behind the loo. There was the spillage, the beer smell, the telling trail of destruction I left behind.

Acute illness didn't hit until I was flying home after a whole year in Japan, with a stopover in London. Looking back, I had long suspected something was seriously wrong with me.

Waiting for the flight at Tokyo Airport, I decided to drink some lager in the loo. I braced myself, shoved the can to my mouth as if it were the barrel of a gun, and gulped down as much of the liquid as I could. One slug, two slugs, three, four, five. As the lager swamped my stomach, I had to wipe sweat from my brow with trembling, clammy fingers. Pausing for breath, I took some more, one, two, three swigs, rest, breathe, until the alcohol attacked my innards anew. The pain in my abdomen smacked as hard as the meanest fist. It was excruciating, spitting flames this way and that, flames spreading down into my burning belly and up through my chest, stealing my ability to breathe. This was pain like no other.

I stood up, leaned against the wall, closed my eyes. As the flames in my stomach subsided, I inhaled a little stale toilet air and felt my gorge rise. Sweat was oozing from pores I didn't even know I had. I grabbed a mirror out of my bag and peered at my face. The person looking back was not me but someone whose lips were smeared with a white paste, aftermath, I assumed, of an antacid 'overdose'.

For once, I was frightened of what I had become. I left the loo and headed for the departure lounge where I sat in silence, arms folded over sore tummy, feeling my insides roar and burn. I felt as if I were being eaten away from the inside. I thought I was going to be sick, held my breath for a minute, gulped and closed my eyes. I always did everything in my power to keep the drink down otherwise the effect wore off too quickly. The nausea relented for a while, leaving me feeling warm, elated; the way I yearned to be all the time. But then there was a sharp pain again, gradually getting worse.

Once on the plane, I fell into a deep sleep; so deep a fellow passenger woke me up to see whether I was all right. I immediately ordered champagne and took a long drink. Two hours to go until landing at Heathrow. Normally, champagne didn't upset me, but this time it did; hitting my stomach afresh, creating a burning sensation, which made me retch. I held my breath again and grabbed some antacid powders from my handbag, swallowing them with another gulp of champagne. Then came an excruciating pain, which sent noisy messages along my nerve endings, saying: 'Stop, please stop drinking.' I started vomiting, spewing into my lap and over the back of the seat in front. The passenger who had helped me moved away in disgust. A hostess took the bottle of champagne away and handed me a white paper bag. I couldn't stop vomiting, every retch accompanied by a stab of red-hot pain which gradually became intolerable. I started moaning, uncontrollably. I was doubled up, my head in my hands, the sickness gone.

I don't remember much about the plane landing, just the ladder down to the ground – and falling down those metallic steps, trying but failing to grab the sides; sinking into an abyss of pain, into a place where everything was black and still.

I lost two weeks out of my life. I found out later I had been rushed by ambulance to a hospital in Plumstead, in south-east London.

When I came round one morning and asked for a cup of tea, I was told by a young nurse that my funeral had been arranged for the following week. I actually laughed when I heard. I phoned home, got a lukewarm response from my mother; delayed shock possibly.

'Oh, Nic,' she said, 'I'm so glad you've rallied.'

My father didn't speak to me, didn't even send a card. None of the family did. They had become so used to me being in hospital that they simply forgot to show any emotion. Or they were ashamed. One alcoholic in the family is bad luck. Two is careless. This latest episode they saw as an all-time low, hitting the gutter, and they weren't going to drag me out. In fact my parents might have preferred to see me disappear down the drain, without a trace.

The doctor in charge of the ward told me I had acute pancreatitis and, by rights, should have died after I collapsed. He said it was a serious though treatable condition, which had one of three causes: gallstones, alcohol, with a third that was unknown. He said it usually happened to older men and was relatively unusual in women, especially young women.

'Please don't take offence, but I need to know how much you drink,' he said politely.

I had already decided I would fall into the 'unknown' category. I told him I didn't drink to excess, maybe a couple of bottles of wine a week. Nobody was going to disagree with me. Looking back, I often wonder whether that 'unknown' category was full of people like me who couldn't face the fact they had a drink problem.

# Chapter 13

# Last Rites

It was Saturday, 16 September 1978. My father was climbing and I'd promised to call round to see my mother, check up on her. When I arrived, I didn't need a key to get into the house – which was unusual because Mummy always locked the outside door when she was in bed, just in case.

Experiencing the usual feeling of anxiety mingled with relief to be home, I went upstairs to the sitting room and sat down heavily in my armchair, desperate to take the weight off my feet. I was fitter since I'd cut down on my drinking six months before, the reality of my medical problems finally hitting home. Nevertheless, if I needed to drink for the psychological boost, I did so, despite vomiting most of it back up. It made me feel ashamed, but that didn't stop me. I finally understood how my mother must have felt all those years.

The house was quiet, lacked life, apart from the odd noise from outside, a snarling dog, a neighbour shouting something, cars in the street. At least when I'd lived at home, there was music. Now there was nothing.

It was lunchtime. I wondered how much my mother would have had to drink today. Eventually, I steeled myself to go and see what state she was in, heading first for the kitchen. There was a huge stack of unwashed dishes by the sink, a few days old by the looks of them. I looked in the fridge and found packets of out-of-date meat. There were letters, unopened, on the worktop. I slid on a chunk of cooking fat, cursed, then looked for the yellow gloves my mother never wore. I noticed how my once-red, chapped, swollen hands had all but returned to normal, living away from this scene of compulsive domesticity. I still liked to clean until my hands were sore, but there wasn't very much dirt in my small home. And there wasn't a nagging need to clean up after Mummy.

I realised I was hungry and, seeing some vegetables in the rack, I stood at the window peeling a few potatoes, putting off the moment I always dreaded. In the garden below, everything looked the same as ever, a few flowers, an assortment of shrubs, roses growing up the trellis, trained by my father's green wiring and carefully pruned. I spotted two crows strutting about the lawn where the grass hadn't been cut for months. One of the birds cawed so loudly, I felt myself shiver.

I pulled my hands out of the soapy water, dried them on a towel, went through and stood outside my mother's bedroom. I opened her door as quietly as I could, my energy sapping with every slow turn of the handle. I stuck my head round and saw the room was as gloomy as ever. Drawn curtains were not unusual in this house, especially in the middle of the afternoon. They were my mother's most forceful statement; testimony to her isolation from the rest of the world.

The first thing I noticed was her bedside lamp lying on the floor, its bulb dead, having burned a hole in the carpet, right through to the wood. I could see the brown patch from where I was standing. It was large, deep and heavily singed. It was lucky nothing had caught fire. Next to it, in a disorganised heap, was my mother.

Her head looked awkward, as if it had been screwed onto her body back to front. She lay on her right side, facing the door, maximum impact guaranteed as usual. The surprise element in a drinker's life tended to inspire the falls, the little accidents. She was wearing her old blue dressing gown, which gaped down the middle, displaying her bruised thighs and bony knees, calves covered in tiny grey-green veins and more bruises. Her arms were outstretched, mouth wide open; saliva running down her chin and down the front of her dressing gown. She had vomited on the carpet, near where the lamp had fallen.

Out of the corner of my unwilling eye, I could see a

mouse waddling across the room, stopping briefly over by the window to perch on hind legs and twitch its nose. I shuddered, wondering how long it had been there. It looked elderly and put upon, the way Mummy had always looked in the days when she had to plod home with her secret stash of booze. The mouse was heading for the wardrobe, moving so slowly I began to think it too was the worse for Smirnoff.

I wanted to go to Mummy but my legs wouldn't move. I clung, instead, to the door for support. I could see two empty bottles of vodka and pills of various colours scattered around her. She was dead. The moment I had been dreading so long was here and I didn't want to know.

I backed out of her room, shut the door with a bang and walked back to the kitchen to finish peeling the potatoes the old-fashioned way, with a knife. I was holding the knife so tightly my knuckles began to ache with the strain, peeling large chunks off the potatoes instead of just removing the skin. The wasted lumps of vegetable were filling the sink along with the salty tears splashing down my cheeks.

'Mummy, I did love you,' the words blocked my throat even as a voice inside my head asked: 'Did you really love her that much?'

'Okay,' I replied, 'I know I really only came home to check she was still alive, but I don't feel guilty. I've promised myself all these years I wouldn't when the time came. It's just that I never expected it to come. You don't. She's been in her room most of the time for the last five years. I did what I could.'

'Did you really?' the inner voice persisted. 'And, pray, what was this "everything" you did? Shouted, bawled, screamed and bullied? Your mother was an alcoholic. That's not a condition to be judged. She was ill. Do you think for one moment you treated her like someone suffering?'

They say guilt is Catholic. I have never thought so. Guilt is what happens when someone loves drink more than they love you. You watch them rotting away in front of you but can't do anything to stop them. It's the acuteness of that feeling, the overwhelming powerlessness, which destroys you in the end. Life shouldn't be that way. You feel it must be your fault for not being lovable enough. I felt guilty all my life, first for leaving the house to go to school and later for trying to make my way in the world. And she died when I was out. I knew she would. If I'd been there, I could have called an ambulance, done something. I wasn't there, though. Nobody was.

I ran back to Mummy's bedroom. Her television, I now noticed, flickered in the background, as if it, too, was contemplating giving up the ghost. How long had she been lying like this?

'Mummy . . . ?' I moved towards her, arms outstretched, bent over and felt for a pulse in her wrist. Nothing. She felt cold, far removed from the warmth she normally exuded when she'd try, after a bottle or two, to kiss me, only to watch me recoil, turn away, then, guiltily, proffer my lips – far too late. The damage had been done, the hurt inflicted. I knelt down, rested my head on her chest and clutched her hand, freezing cold, pressing my ear against her mouth, just to double-check she wasn't breathing.

I walked over to pull back the curtains, careful not to look at the mouse, by now huddled in a corner, whiskers twitching. When I drew the curtains, the room still looked dingy. I inhaled the musty smell, customary stink of drink and drugs, and made my way back to the door, pausing at her handbag that was lying at the foot of her unmade bed. I picked it up, delved inside for her creamy wallet, stuffed with fivers. I grabbed a handful of notes, my habit, my compensation, then closed the bag and carried on to the door, stopped again, this time at her dressing table. I looked at the pink face powder gathered in clumps beneath the glass top, at its orange-and-cream container with the filthy compact puff she was always dropping on the floor. I looked at the silver hairbrushes, and the familiarity of it all made me ache. I put the fivers back down. I didn't need to hurt her any more. I felt the saddest I have ever felt in my life, such a complex mixture of emotions.

For some reason, I turned on the light before leaving her room, then went down a few stairs, opened a door to the back garden, stumbled down some stone steps to the outside where I knelt down on the lawn, in the uncut grass, my head in my hands. I don't know how long I stayed like that, sobbing, but I eventually remembered my father, stood up and went back into the house to phone him.

The dining room seemed miles away. I thought I would never reach it. When I did, I sat down at the table and dialled his number. He answered straight away. His 'Hello' provoked nothing but silence in me as I summoned a voice from sixty million feet beneath the floorboards.

'Daddy,' my voice was thick as cold porridge. He seemed pleased to hear from me, until I dropped my bombshell: 'Mummy's dead,' I said.

I know I should have eased the blow, but this was the best I could manage. He told me to call our GP or an ambulance, said he would come as quickly as he could. He also told me to stay in the dining room until he arrived, as if he thought I couldn't cope without him there. Irritated, I slammed the receiver back down and sat staring out of the window at the grey clouds gathering over the nearby hills. My mother was dead.

The morning of the funeral was sunless, damp and grey. I kept shivering even though it wasn't cold. I was standing at the entrance to the churchyard on a pathway of crunchy gravel. The small church had stained-glass windows, one or two in need of repair. It looked as if it would be as cold inside as out; a place built for worship, not comfort. Richard, Michael and I had agreed to meet my father at the door half an hour before the ceremony. Peter was away on holiday and none of us had been able to contact him.

I had chosen to wear French navy, a knee-length skirt and jacket. Mummy would have hated me in black. A large number of people had already gathered outside and were standing politely in groups of two or three. Most were dressed in dark colours; more women than men, more oddballs than straights. In death, she was more popular than she'd ever been alive. Seeing so many people lifted our spirits briefly, especially Richard's.

I felt as if I were at a cocktail party, as if I should circulate and tell everyone what a wonderful person my mother had been – although they must have known that or they wouldn't have been here. I recognised some patients from the Crichton as well as her psychiatrist who looked very old and cried into a white hankie. There were relatives, aunts and uncles, the odd cousin. It struck me as sad that I didn't really know any of them well. Drink had kept us all apart: the Barrys safe in our solitary shame; them, mostly content to keep our dysfunction at arm's length.

I stood, looking at the gravel underfoot. I still couldn't believe Mummy was dead. If she were here, we'd be bitching about everybody, deploring their fashion sense, as if we had some reason to sit in judgement. But she wouldn't be here, even if she were alive, I corrected myself. She'd be at home drunk, lying in the bath or on her bed, and I'd be chivvying her as usual, ordering her from room to room, irritating her as much as a pebble in her shoe.

'I'm so sorry.' A woman, her face partially hidden by a large hat, put an arm around my shoulder. 'I suppose it was for the best,' she added before gliding away, as if across some invisible ballroom. Just as well she had moved away or I might have thumped her. What did that mean, 'for the best'? Was death a release to someone who had existed in a dirty bedroom for five years, too afraid to venture out without a bellyful of booze, despised as a drunkard, yet a formidable woman in her time? Was she rushing around Heaven now, sober, cured of all hang-ups and hangovers, able suddenly to meet people without the help of her lifelong crutch? Other people said her death was 'a blessing'. For whom, I wondered? Them? Was it a blessing because they no longer had to tolerate this supposedly snooty woman in their midst who betrayed her class, let the side down? She had needed releasing in life, not death.

Another woman approached me, smiling, arm extended.

'You must be Nicola,' she said, clasping my hand warmly. I nodded.

'Your mother saved my life.' It was said so matter-of-factly.

'How d'you mean?'

'I met her at an AA meeting, my first one, years ago. I was really out of it. When I think of it now, I . . .' she blushed. 'The next morning, when I woke up, I vowed never to go there again but your mother talked me into going back and I've been attending ever since. She didn't just preach at me, she was actually there to meet me, at the door, never left my side. She didn't care when I phoned her, any time of the day or night – at least, until she started drinking again. I never saw her after that.' The woman looked down, frowning. 'I was so upset when I heard she'd died. We all were. We felt guilty, because the Fellowship didn't work for her. It doesn't suit everybody, you see. You've got to want it, badly. But she was a marvellous person. You must have been so proud of her, Nicola, as she was of you. She was always going on about you.'

She stopped talking for a moment then added: 'The thing about drink is that it prevents people from loving. It takes over their lives, their emotions and they're not able to function at a normal level. I hope you know what I mean. I bet you thought your mother didn't care about you. I know different. I know how much she really did care.'

The woman backed away. 'Anyway, I won't keep you. Not today. It's just that I was so lucky to have met her when I did.' She started crying – right there outside the church, tears ran down her cheeks, over her smart grey coat. 'I wish I could have helped her in return.'

I caught sight of my father approaching. The woman looked at him through dark, slightly suspicious eyes, but checked herself. She held out her hand and shook his.

'Claude? Claude Barry?' she queried.

'That's me,' Daddy replied, charming as ever.

'I've heard a lot about you.'

He didn't make any wisecracks, but shook her hand then turned to me. He was on time, for a change, neatly dressed in a dark suit, white shirt and black tie. He looked more surprised than sad, as if he hadn't been expecting anybody to turn up. He gave me his usual, perfunctory, trying-to-be-fatherly peck on the cheek then moved off to speak to someone called Brian, a colleague.

I suddenly recalled him standing outside Mummy's room the day after her death, a week ago. I had tried to comfort him, asked how he was feeling. It seemed for a moment that he was going to open up, respond. Then he said: 'I felt bad yesterday but I'm over it now.' That was it, the end of thirty years or so of marriage. It was typical.

He never talked to me again about Mummy dying.

The mourners were heading towards the door, some at

a loss for words. The people who did speak to us were the ones none of us knew. Richard recognised a couple.

'Who are all these people?' I asked my father.

He shook his head. 'I was about to ask you the same thing.'

Daddy stood back to let us go in first, then followed through the door of the old chapel. Inside the vestibule, the walls and ceiling were sallow with age. To our right, an old man with a shaky hand was trying to light some candles on a table. Two men stood on opposite sides of an inner door, handing out sheets of prayers and hymns. We walked into the chapel to a glorious blast of Bach's organ music and found more people already seated inside.

As I sat down near the front, I noticed two women kneeling in pews on the opposite side of the church. Something made them stand out: their reddish-purple faces and pockmarked skin. AA, I guessed. The one nearest me had thick grey hair down to her waist. It hung in clumps and looked as if it had never seen a comb. She wore a long brown coat and tackety boots, the sort a troubled teenager might wear to destroy telephone kiosks. The women were passing something backwards and forwards between them. It was a while before I realised it was a bag of sweets. They were sucking boiled sweets in church like most people did at the cinema. It was something I'd noticed at AA meetings, people replacing drink with sweets. The woman with the tackety boots caught me staring and gave me a look, beguiling, almost challenging. When I smiled, she grinned back then dropped her eyes before sitting down on the wooden bench.

I was distracted by the sight of a man in his thirties, brown hair, parted in the middle, high cheekbones and a full mouth turned up at the corners into a permanent half smile. He stood out in a light-blue denim jacket, zipped up the front, over black trousers and a pair of dark sneakers. He kept looking at the coffin that stood in front of the altar, wiping his eyes with a large white handkerchief. At one point, when he held the hankie to his face, I noticed he was wearing pink nail varnish. His hands were immaculate, long pianist's fingers and bony wrists. I suddenly realised who he was – Thomas, Mummy's transvestite friend. She told me they had become very close. I remembered the day Thomas had answered the ad she put in *The Scotsman* for her designer wear, the one who'd wanted clothes for his disabled aunt. Or, rather, for himself.

In the pew kneeling ncxt to Thomas was a tall woman with long, dark, wavy hair, wearing trousers and a black duffle coat with the collar pulled right up at the back. I had no idea who she was, although she seemed to know Thomas well and kept putting her arm around his shoulders.

I started sobbing. Why hadn't I seen the good in my mother when all these people obviously had? Why hadn't she and I been able to help each other? How was I going to cope with standing outside the church, listening to words of commiseration from so many strangers? I was glad that, for once in my life, I was sober.

My father looked momentarily mortified by my tears, which made me cry even louder. I could see him thinking, 'For God's sake, the funeral hasn't even started yet.'

A business-like priest appeared out of nowhere, knelt down at the altar and clasped his hands together in prayer. I recognised him as Monsignor Conway whom she had known from her days at the Crichton, one of the gentlest men I had ever met: devout, intensely human, unfailingly warm. My mother adored him, and he had been a good friend to her over the years. Whether she phoned drunk or sober, he always listened.

We all joined in the Mass responses, some more knowledgeable of Catholicism than others. I followed the missal at my seat, sung the hymns and listened to three readings. The woman with the long grey hair stood up and strode to the front of the church to give a reading. She was from AA and read an extract from the Big Book.

I noticed my father was shaking. He surely wasn't going to cry. I don't think I could have handled that. He stood, rigid, expressionless, throughout the Mass, clutching the back of the seat in front until his knuckles whitened. I kept looking at him. To think he had once doted on his wife but turned his back on her when she 'let him down'.

After the Mass, as we walked back down the aisle to the door, I drew myself up, put my shoulders back and held my head high. I wanted my mother to leave this world with some dignity; a state of mind she had never managed to acquire in life.

I had promised I would take her to be buried alongside her parents and the brother she had worshipped, in the south of England. So, a few days later, I drove all the way, with her ashes in a large box on the passenger seat, to an old Sussex village, close to where she had lived as a little girl. There, I met Peter and Lindsay. A vicar greeted us and led us in a brief ceremony. As we stood in that charming churchyard, reflecting sadly on my mother's life, I vowed that, whatever happened, I was not going to waste my life in the way she had wasted hers. No matter how hard it proved, no matter how long it took, I would not allow myself to sink into drink and drugs. I was going to live my life to the full. It was the greatest tribute I could have paid a woman I felt I had not loved enough. What saddened me most wasn't the years I had spent looking after my mother but the fact that, in the end, it had all come to nothing.

When the vicar sprinkled some holy water over the

family grave, just to the left of a weeping willow, I had a brief notion to add a few drops of vodka but decided, with a real surge of relief, that she wouldn't need it where she was going.

# Afterword

After my mother died, I saw my father occasionally, but he became more and more isolated, difficult to reach, making my visits home more nerve-wracking than ever. The house was perpetually dark and gloomy; the rooms bereft, my mother's sick room left untouched. Although the place had always been unhappy, it had possessed some spark of life, even if it was only the sheer unpredictability of the situation within. My father now treated the house like a caravan, returning there to sleep after a day's walking or the private work he had done since retiring some years earlier.

Soon after the funeral, he spent some money, on new furniture coverings, on painting the hall, on a new car: putting his house in order. At the same time, he started whittering on about how he wanted to 'go' on the hill. It was, he maintained, the only way to die. He didn't go mountaineering as often, possibly he didn't feel the need to get away, now that the main source of his anguish had gone. He wasn't any happier after Mummy's death. It was as if her sickness had given him a role in life; duties to carry out.

My father changed his will shortly before he died. His lawyer never told us what the change entailed; only commented on the strange timing, one week before his death. My father made one further amendment. Richard was due home from Australia the weekend Daddy had planned to climb Cairn Toul in the Cairngorms. He put it off until the following weekend so he would see Richard, his favourite, before he went off on his jaunt. At that time, he was taking beta-blockers for angina and must have known how serious his condition was. He knew that Cairn Toul, at more than 4,000ft, was accessible only through prolonged physical effort. He did his preparations, said his goodbyes as usual and went off to tackle the mountain with three of his climbing cronies. They stopped for lunch at the summit, had a leisurely picnic and my father said that it had been his most memorable day ever on the hill.

As they began their descent, after about ten minutes, one of his friends, Donald, noticed my father was missing – had fallen off the end of their group. He described to me afterwards how he had braced himself against the wind and walked back, surprised, since he had never before known Claude to lag behind. On the contrary, my father was often first up and first down. He had done a lot of stopping on this day, ostensibly to admire the view. When Donald reached the peak, he saw a distant figure etched against the skyline; a nondescript, elderly man in a grey anorak, perched, oddly, on a stone protruding conveniently from the rock face, rucksack by his side, head tilted back, mouth wide open. As Donald approached, he noticed one of Claude's eyes was shut, the other stared out into the bleak distance, unblinking. It was obvious he was dead.

Donald grabbed him by the shoulders, cleared his airways, placed his mouth over my father's and blew into the lips, simultaneously massaging the area around his heart. No response, nothing. Eventually, he undid my father's rucksack, searched for the bivvy bag he always carried and manhandled my father inside it, then ignoring the tears gathering behind his eyes, began his descent. Years later, he told me he never recovered from the shock. They hadn't exactly been friends but the relationship with Donald was possibly the closest I ever saw my father get to anybody.

Richard and I were at home talking when the doorbell rang. It was approaching midnight. Two policemen stood on the doorstep, an air of apology about them. One said: 'Could we come in?' Once inside, the same officer said: 'It's Dr Barry. I'm afraid he died earlier today on Cairn Toul.'

*

The funeral was well attended, almost stately, and people said polite things. When it was all over I took stock of my parentless life. I moved out to a small cottage in Cramond and began a career as a freelance journalist, something I had long been thinking about. I was beginning to drink a lot again and lived in terror of the pancreatic pain returning. After a year, I turned to AA for help and stopped drinking very quickly, despite finding it impossible to agree with the organisation's rigid views on alcoholism, the meetings I was supposed to attend, the staying away from the first drink a day at a time. It seemed to be a case of one size fits all. There was more to the illness than stopping drinking. Take away the bottle and the battle remains. Take away the bottle and all my insecurities were still there. How to tackle that? However, I was convinced I had conquered the drinking aspect of my problems when I didn't turn back to it in 1982, after I was given the worst news of my life.

After my father's funeral, I asked Richard if he would stop climbing. He said. 'No' with such vehemence I never dared raise the subject again. I also asked him why he climbed. 'It's the closest I'll ever get to a spiritual life,' was his immediate and unhesitating answer. He took a pleasure in it that I wasn't getting from anything, not even the bottle. Despite what had happened to Daddy, I couldn't deny him that.

One day, when he had gone climbing in Glencoe, he didn't return to his flat, and I became aware of a feeling of mild unease. I phoned a friend, who said the chances of a mountaineering accident happening twice in the same family were one in a million. I took some comfort from that.

I had seen Richard the day before quite by accident, crossing the road near Edinburgh Royal Infirmary, where he was working as an anaesthetist. He had a broad grin on his face, his white coat flapping along behind him like a lazy companion. He looked so happy, so engrossed in life he didn't notice me tooting my horn. That moment will remain engraved in my mind forever, a snapshot I hang onto from a past I'd rather forget. I never saw him again.

It was nearly midnight when the police car drew up outside my house. I knew straight away, just by the faces of the officers coming up the path what had happened. After all, it was only a few years since my father had died. I walked, almost strode, to the front door, knowing only too well the life-altering, heart-stopping moment waiting behind it.

One of the two policemen steered me gently into the living room. He swallowed, steeled himself: 'It's Dr Barry,' he said, just as they had said the last time, when my father had died three years earlier.

'I am sorry to have to tell you that your brother is dead.'

Richard had fallen 400ft down a rock face in the mountains and his camera had been found inches away from his body. To take a photo, he had momentarily put down his ice axe, somehow managing to create his own avalanche.

On that blackest of black days, four climbers had died, three on Ben Nevis, a fourth found in a corrie in Glencoe, killed by an avalanche on Am Bodach. The fourth climber was my brother.

Up until then, I had only ever seen avalanches on television. I knew they involved vast amounts of snow and ice, the sort which slides, sweeps, rages and tumbles; the sort which smashes heads against rocks and pins bodies to cliff surfaces. Not for nothing do climbers refer to an avalanche as 'the white death'.

As the relative of a dead climber, you are left out in the cold. The police do not rush to your door with the news. You usually see it on TV first, hear that a climber has died on the same mountain your relative is on. No names until the family have been informed. They show the mountain and the rescue team in action, the helicopters, the snow and the ice. You hear 'experts' discussing the deaths, but, still, nobody tells you anything, until that chilling knock on the door. It happens so quickly, yet unbearably slowly as well. To a certain extent, that is always the way with sudden death. There's no preparation, no time to repair relationships if they are fractured, no chance to say goodbye or thank you for being such a good brother; just the numbness, the unanswered questions and the trauma of life without Richard. The only real involvement my other brothers and I had was scattering the ashes of both my father and Richard on their favourite mountain, Bidean Nam Bian in Glencoe; a cold, inhospitable place, all scree and rocks and uphill slog; almost ghostly, eerily empty. No wonder Glencoe translates as the Vale of Weeping.

I have always missed my mother, wish I could see her now and bring her up to date with my life. Her death wasn't, on the face of it, as heroic as one in the mountains, yet it touched me far more deeply. I'm glad she was spared the agony of losing Richard. But on 7 July and 15 February respectively, I think of my father and my precious brother, of how they kept running away from home and of how much they enjoyed their escape.

I never went back to drinking again. Occasionally, I start a glass of wine but rarely finish it. I don't like being with people who drink and am very intolerant of drunks. I joined the *Edinburgh Evening News* in 1990 as a feature writer, loved the work but, despite doing well, struggled with the lifestyle. Moving from newspaper to newspaper, I fell foul of a number of Scottish editors, apart from a couple who managed to make use of my weirdness. I was an editor myself, briefly, of *The Big Issue*, discovering the vendors were soulmates and admired the sheer effort they put into existing, especially those on methadone, who, daily, had to travel long distances to collect their supply.

My saviour, Alastair Murray, was one of the few good experiences to come out of working on the *Daily Record* in Glasgow. It was 1997 and the more he saw of my life, the more he was open-mouthed in disbelief. I didn't have a TV, didn't have a washing machine, didn't go away on holiday. He thought me totally deprived, said he would introduce me to the twenty-first century and taught me how to let my hair down. With his extraordinarily generous nature, he learned to cope with my mood swings and insecurities. We live in a beautiful graveyard in Edinburgh, overlooking a woodland dell, the Water of Leith and dead bodies aplenty, the best neighbours I have ever had. We have a dog we adore, a Westie called Coll, who brings even more warmth into our relationship. We also have Alastair's two daughters, Joanne and Hazel, and their wonderful boyfriends, now their husbands, Hugh and Richard and granddaughter Erin with one more on the way. They are the family I never imagined I'd have, couldn't picture myself co-habiting with, sharing life with, being normal with.

It would be good if I could say everything was perfect

but accuracy demands I admit that occasional shadows lurk within the light, however bright it happens to be shining. Even though the longer I live with Alastair, the more the light prevails, there are dark, dark times, when chance remarks wound to an unbearable degree, when I revert to sobbing uncontrollably; something I never did as a child when it might have been more appropriate.

Alastair likes to describe me as 'the last of the cheap nights out', meaning whenever we go out for a meal I take one sip of the wine then hand the rest over to him in exchange for his car keys. I was never an alcoholic in any physical sense. That is, physically my body did not crave alcohol, and drinking did not agree with me. Not that definitions matter. Mentally, I couldn't function without it. It enabled me to be somebody else, to be anyone in the world but me. Drink represented a battle my mother had fought, lost, then passed onto me.

My mother is still here, has been here down the years, an absent presence, the sort you find in a haunted house. Even when she was present during my childhood, she was absent. Yet she managed and is still managing to exert a powerful influence over my life. During the good times as well as the bad, she lives on like a faint but persistent echo.

Now you can buy any of these other bestselling non-fiction titles from your bookshop or *direct from the publisher*.

## FREE P&P AND UK DELIVERY
(Overseas and Ireland £3.50 per book)

**Pete Doherty: My Prodigal Son**    Jacqueline Doherty    £6.99
Nothing can break a mother's love for her only son. The mother of Britain's most notorious drug addict talks for the first time about what she calls 'the Peter problem' in a deeply moving account of his very public self-destruction, and her endless love and hope for him.

**For the Love of My Mother**    John Rodgers    £6.99
The harrowing but ultimately uplifting tale of a young woman who, though consigned to a Magdalene Laundry and separated from her baby son, resolves never to give up on life in the hope of being reunited with him once more.

**Don't Wake Me at Doyles**    Maura Murphy    £7.99
The remarkable memoir of an ordinary Irish woman and her extraordinary life. From her early days running wild in the countryside, to her destructive marriage to a hard-working, hard-drinking womaniser, the birth of her nine children, and a life-or-death choice that would change her forever.

**Life, Interrupted**    James McConnel    £6.99
A memoir of obsession, compulsion, loneliness, alcoholism, music, the quest for identity, the search for love, some very fine jokes and late-diagnosed Tourette's.

**The Boy with No Shoes**    William Horwood    £6.99
This heartbreaking story of a boy's struggle with early trauma is based on William Horwood's own remarkable childhood in an English coastal town after the Second World War. Using all the skills evident in his modern classics, he has written an inspiring tale of a journey from a past too painful to imagine to the future every child deserves.

**Daddy's Little Girl**    Julia Latchem-Smith    £6.99
The powerful story of a little girl's sexual abuse at the hands of the father she loved and trusted, and of her triumph as a young woman in seeing him convicted for his crime.

To order, simply call 01235 400 414
visit our website: www.headline.co.uk
or email orders@bookpoint.co.uk

Prices and availability subject to change without notice.